ENDORSEMENTS

"*A Time for Confidence* has all the hallmarks we have come to expect from its author: an enviable grasp of history, shrewdness in analyzing our culture, and a deep sense that God's Word has lost nothing of its ancient power. Amid what may feel like the shifting of tectonic plates under Western society, and facing the danger of discouragement, we want Steve Nichols near at hand to point us to a safe place to stand. But he does more than that in these pages. Far from letting us lose heart, he shows us that the gospel gives us many more reasons for confidence than for despair. *A Time for Confidence* is both a tract and a tonic for ou

:LAIR B. FERGUSON
Ligonier Ministries

"Christians a.. ....g .. ..st complex times in human history. Our culture is in the midst of a moral and intellectual revolution, the pace of which is unprecedented in human history. The moral reasoning that has stood as the foundation of Western civilization is being upended, and those who once stood out as voices of moral clarity are now ostracized as intellectual outlaws on the wrong side of history. But, as Stephen Nichols makes clear in this book, this is no time for panic. *A Time for Confidence* is a needed reminder that in the midst of the cultural revolution, Christians can be confident that our sovereign God still reigns over human history. Indeed, Christians can also be confident that the church militant will one day be the church triumphant. If you find yourself wavering in the face of cultural opposition, let this book spur you on to greater faithfulness and confidence in the reigning and risen Christ."

—R. ALBERT MOHLER JR.
President, The Southern Baptist Theological Seminary
Louisville, Ky.

A TIME FOR

CONFIDENCE

TRUSTING GOD IN A
POST-CHRISTIAN SOCIETY

STEPHEN J. NICHOLS

ℝ *Reformation Trust*   A DIVISION OF LIGONIER MINISTRIES, ORLANDO, FL

A Time for Confidence: Trusting God in a Post-Christian Society

© 2016 by Stephen J. Nichols

Published by Reformation Trust Publishing
A division of Ligonier Ministries
421 Ligonier Court, Sanford, FL 32771
Ligonier.org   ReformationTrust.com

Printed in Ann Arbor, Michigan
Cushing-Malloy, Inc.
November 2016
First edition

ISBN 978-1-56769-720-9 (Paperback)
ISBN 978-1-56769-756-8 (ePub)
ISBN 978-1-56769-757-5 (Kindle)

Cover design: Vanessa Ayala
Interior design and typeset: Katherine Lloyd, The DESK

Scripture quotations are from the ESV® Bible (The Holy Bible, English Standard Version®), copyright © 2001 by Crossway, a publishing ministry of Good News Publishers. Used by permission. All rights reserved.

Library of Congress Cataloging-in-Publication Data

Names: Nichols, Stephen J., 1970- author.
Title: A time for confidence : trusting God in a post-Christian society / Stephen J. Nichols.
Description: Orlando, FL : Reformation Trust Publishing, 2016.
Identifiers: LCCN 2016028434 | ISBN 9781567697209
Subjects: LCSH: Trust in God--Christianity. | Faith. | Christianity and culture.
Classification: LCC BV4637 .N53 2016 | DDC 261--dc23
LC record available at https://lccn.loc.gov/2016028434

CONTENTS

Though an army encamp against me,
my heart shall not fear;
though war arise against me,
yet I will be confident.

—PSALM 27:3

Chapter One

A TIME FOR
CONFIDENCE

One day in May 1995 changed the life of Henry Wanyoike forever. He was all of twenty-one years old, and like many of his fellow Kenyans, he dreamed of making his mark as a distance runner and becoming a national hero. He had a 5K time of 13:50. That is less than 10 seconds away from the 2012 Olympic gold medal time. Distance runners don't peak until their late twenties, thirties, or even forties. At twenty-one, Wanyoike appeared to be headed for a bright future as one of Kenya's running superstars. Then, that one day, he had a stroke and lost his sight.

Depressed and disillusioned, Wanyoike drifted for the next several years. He was a lost soul. He went to a school for the blind in Machokos, Kenya. An administrator at the school knew of his running past and saw his flailing present, so he suggested that Wanyoike take up running again. Within a few years, Wanyoike had set world records at the Paralympics and at the World Championships in the 5K and 10K.

In 2005, he had phenomenal back-to-back marathon performances. Over 26.2 miles of the streets of London, he set a world record, finishing in 2:31:31. However, he didn't have much time to celebrate—or recover. Seven days later, he broke his own record at the Hamburg Marathon in Germany.

He has since held political office and has established a foundation for the disabled in Kenya. He has singlehandedly contributed to raising awareness of the disabled in his country and has helped many formerly marginalized people find places where they can contribute. He also continues to train, with the goal of breaking his own records leading him on. In a nation of superstar runners, Wanyoike has taken a prominent place among their ranks.

Runner's World magazine featured the life story of Henry Wanyoike, calling him a visionary. When he first started running again after his stroke, he stumbled and fell a lot—even with guides to help him. With his sight gone, he was afraid. But he learned that there is something far better that sight. Michelle Hamilton, referring to something Wanyoike had said, put it this way: "Vision, as [Wanyoike] likes to point out, is more powerful than sight."[1]

What we need today, more than sight, is vision. Seeing, in our day, easily leads to fear. In fact, this has been the case through most of the ages. One of the things that separated the prophets of Israel from the people of Israel was the difference between sight and vision. The people saw the temporal, and they could not get past what they were seeing. God granted the prophets vision of the eternal, which towered above and overshadowed the temporal.

Where the people of Israel saw problems, Israel's prophets saw God and His promises. Where the people saw allurements and temptations, the prophets saw God's call to purity and God's call to covenant obedience. Where the people mistook the shadows for the eternal and abiding reality, the prophets saw beyond the shadows and saw straight into the truly real.

If we only see what appears before us, we may easily shrink back in fear, or, worse, drift away from our first love. We can be enticed away by appearances. The book of Proverbs offers vivid accounts of the destruction that comes in the wake of being fooled by alluring sights. Seeing can lead to our ruin. Instead, we need to cultivate our vision.

Vision led Wanyoike to make a difference for his fellow disabled Kenyans, and it led him to break world records. Vision leads to accomplishments. Sight often keeps us from even getting to the starting line. Wanyoike lost his sight, but he gained vision. Sight takes us off the path; vision keeps us pressing on toward the goal.

Today, we need vision. We need not be pulled down, distressed, or disillusioned by what we see. This is a time for confidence.

Cower, Capitulate, or Cave?

This is not a time to cower. There is plenty of temptation to do so, especially if we're too busy seeing and we lack vision.

Advocates of same-sex agendas and so-called gender benders have pressed their issues through the courts, through legislatures, and through popular media with a vengeance. The speed with which both public opinion and social policy have made a 180-degree turn on these issues is unprecedented. We are experiencing cultural whiplash.

Even TV commercials are not safe. A 2015 television ad for Chobani yogurt has a woman waking up and enjoying a cup of yogurt in bed. Before she leaves and wraps herself in the sheet, she playfully runs her finger along the foot of the other person in bed with her. As the commercial ends, we see that the other person turns out to be a woman. In another commercial, Wells Fargo happily lends money to two mommies as they adopt a child. This is nothing less than an attempt to normalize a formerly culturally marginalized view.

Macklemore and Ryan Lewis' 2012 rap song "Same Love" mainstreamed same-sex relationships in rap music. Kacey Musgraves' "Follow Your Arrow" brought lyrics that extol same-sex relationships to the bastion of God and old-fashioned values: country music. In 2014, it won Song of the Year at the Country Music Awards, prompting one headline to read "A gay-loving, weed-smoking anthem just won country music's Song of the Year."

U.S. Supreme Court Justice Anthony Kennedy has thundered that gay marriage is a noble purpose. Centering his argument on "dignity," he has expressed shock at the narrowness of any opinion that dissents from the recognition of gay marriage. To be pro-gay is to be pro-human dignity, the new legal argument goes. U.S. Supreme Court justices also unfortunately practice what they adjudicate. Back in 2013, Justice Ruth Bader Ginsburg and retired Justice Sandra Day O'Connor presided over separate gay marriage ceremonies held in the Supreme Court Building itself.

A Time of Change

The changes are rapid and systemic, and they can lead one to feel utterly disoriented. Same-sex relationships are mainstreamed, the stuff of commercials, rap songs, country music, and Supreme Court decisions and ceremonies. The pressure on dissenters is enormous. The exertion of power to force this agenda is nearly unprecedented in American history. This could be a time to cower. But it is not.

This is not a time to capitulate. David Gushee, a Southern Baptist theologian and ethicist, once wrote against homosexuality. Then he changed his mind. Progressive pastor and author Brian MacLaren changed his mind. Rob Bell bowed before the idol of Oprah. Here's what he told a national audience on her "Super Soul Sunday": "I think the culture is already there and the church will continue to be even more irrelevant when it quotes letters from two thousand years ago as their best defense."

It's time for the church to catch up, Bell says. In order to do so, we need to look past ancient letters. Instead of looking at the dusty pages of the Bible, we need to look "in front of you [at] the flesh-and-blood people who . . . love each other and just want to go through life with someone."[2]

Ignore the Bible. It's irrelevant to life in the twenty-first century. Capitulate to culture and cultural norms and cultural pressures. The culture is there. Let's catch up, Bell tells us, joined by a tragically growing number of others. Bell can only see the surface. The present culture is blocking his vision.

These are only individuals. But entire Protestant denominations and Christian institutions are also choosing the predilections of culture over God's Holy Word. They care more about the drumbeat of our day than the very words of God. When we see so many people changing their views, it can look like a time to capitulate. But it's not.

This is not a time to cave. In North American contexts, we have far more exposure to adherents of other religions than people did at any other time in our history. When the founders of the United States spoke of religious freedom, they were mainly talking to Protestants, a few Roman Catholics, and a few Jews. Islam was an ocean away. Eastern religions were farther still. Consider the multiplex of religions present in any given suburban neighborhood. What does it mean to live in a religiously plural society?

One rather loud voice tells us it means tolerance. And that means, above all, no room for an exclusive view. How can you be neighborly and think your sincere, even kind, neighbor who happens to follow another religion is bound for hell? It is a time for pluralism, we are told.

Adding to this, we are told that truth is a rather elastic concept. Better to use a lower case and the plural rather than the upper case and the singular—that is, it's better to speak of *truths* than *the Truth*. Even reality itself is up for grabs. For many today, whether due to postmodernism or the onslaught of all things "virtual," reality is seen as a self-construct. I make and shape reality, and I am at the center of the reality I have shaped. There are no laws, no givens, no absolutes. Truth and even reality are social or individual constructs.

In the wake of the 2015 Supreme Court decision in *Obergefell v. Hodges*, which legalized same-sex marriage across the United States, many pundits pointed out that the affirming justices followed public opinion, not strict legal guidelines. They ruled based on the ebb and flow of popular sentiment. One dissenting justice referred to the language of Justice Kennedy's so-called argument as sounding like "a fortune cookie."[3] Public opinion replaced the rule of law. Sentiment trumped legal argument.

The social implications of this are staggering. Marriage is whatever we want it to be. Human life is defined however we want it defined. Gender is a moving target. We have plunged ourselves into a whirlpool of relativism, and we're spiraling toward the drain.

How can the idea of truth, truth as absolute and objective reality, penetrate this new worldview?

Let's put the matter differently. To those who have been shaped by pluralism and postmodernism, advocates of *the Truth* appear as aliens from outer space. Perhaps even better, they appear as throwbacks to the medieval era. Advocates of truth are deemed dangerous in our new cultural climate.

It can seem like a time to cave. But it's not.

All of this only scratches the surface of the circumstances in which we live. This is our cultural moment; this is our time. Enormous pressure to cower, to capitulate, and to cave closes in on us like the unstoppable walls of a compactor. We see it. We sense it.

We have long ago passed the sign that warns of dangerous rapids ahead. We are squarely in the midst of them, frothing and foaming and threatening.

A Time of Confusion

I hadn't used my GPS device in a few years. Like most, I switched to simply using my phone. On one particular trip, though, I brought out my old GPS device for nostalgia's sake. I found it stored away in a closet, dusted it off, and plugged it into to the cigarette lighter. The problem was, I hadn't updated it—ever. Not once from the time I bought it. The maps had long swaths of green where a new highway now ran. It was confused. I was confused.

Similarly, in our rapidly changing society, we are traversing new highways over unfamiliar terrain. Lines have been crossed. Clear boundaries have been rubbed away. It's enough to leave even the casual observer scratching his head in bewilderment. We might feel like we live in an entirely new and altogether strange world.

Confusion means disorientation. It causes one not to think clearly. Confusion can even evolve into a medical condition. This state of confusion rings of tumult, even chaos. It leaves its victim debilitated.

Another nuance to the word *confusion* concerns uncertainty.

Uncertainty can stem from a lack of understanding or from an inability to sift through a cascade of data and information. Such uncertainty can be debilitating. Consider an army—it plans and advances based on clarity of purpose and mission and on certainty of intelligence. Specialists gather, interpret, and transmit information. Commanders sort through it all, drawing on their collective wisdom and experience, and then devise a strategy and give orders. Soldiers, trained and ready, launch into action. From beginning to end, the army that advances does so with a stunning certainty and clarity. A confused army is a defeated army.

We sense the confusion of our moment, the jumbling of categories. Sociologists have taken to using the term *cultural confusion*. The idea here is the loss of consensus, and with a loss of consensus comes a loss of a public ethic, public civility, and public virtue. We have become unable to tell right from wrong—sometimes, we even punish the right. We are awash in a sea of moral uncertainty and relativist ethics. That may even be a generous description. Even seas have boundaries.

You could say we have lost our moral compass. Without that moral compass, we find ourselves bewildered, disoriented, and confused.

How do we respond? What are we to make of the church's mission in this cultural moment?

Chicken Little Lives Here

I suppose many have taken the route of Chicken Little. Remember him?

In British versions of the tale, the main character is named Henny Penny. An acorn drops on the head of Henny Penny (or Chicken Little). We get the impression that this fowl is rather excitable. Immediately, Chicken Little thinks a piece of the sky has fallen. Then, that little thought gets pulled through to its "logical" conclusion. So, Chicken Little runs around telling everyone in sight that the sky is falling. The world is coming to an end.

Jerome was a bit like Chicken Little. Jerome was a late fourth- and early fifth-century scholar and church father. Eusebius Sophrinius Hieronymus—Jerome for short—was born in 347 in the Roman province of Dalmatia, in modern-day Slovenia. He showed brilliance as a young man, so he was sent off to Rome to study. His love of scholarship, not to mention the cloud of a scandal, sent him to the great ancient libraries at Alexandria and Caesarea. He is best known for his Latin translation of the Bible, called the Vulgate.

He spent the last year of his life near Bethlehem, dying in a cave.

When word of the sack of Rome by the Visigoths reached Jerome, he played Chicken Little. Jerome learned that in the mayhem surrounding the sack of Rome, a pious and well-known woman named Marcella, a former acquaintance of Jerome's, died. Jerome took her death to portend far worse things to come. He took Marcella's death as a sign of the death of Rome. Jerome took the death of Rome as a sign of the end of the world. Life as he knew it was crashing down. He started sending letters to his friends warning them that the end was near. In one of those letters, he mourned, "My voice sticks in my throat and, as I dictate, sobs choke my utterance. The City which had taken the whole world was itself taken."[4] In another he wrote, "The world sinks into ruin: Yes!" The sky has fallen.

To be fair, the centuries after the sack of Rome were bleak. The centuries under Rome, however, were not all that sterling, either. More importantly, the world survived the sack of Rome; it even survived the Middle Ages. The sky hadn't fallen after all.

Jerome's fear that the end of the world had come had an ironic shortsightedness to it. His own work survived and thrived through the centuries. Jerome's Vulgate survived. In fact, it had a full eleven centuries' run until Greek texts and translations in common languages such as German and English supplanted it during the time of the Reformation. Jerome's assessment of what he saw happening was wide of the mark. He miscalculated.

It is understandable how easy it could be to play the role of Chicken Little today. We might be tempted to say, "The world sinks into ruin." The Supreme Court is against us; what can we possibly do? Should we all hide in a cave? That is not a healthy response. We can little afford to be Chicken Littles today.

Lack of Confidence

I once had a swimming coach who didn't talk much. He observed. Carefully and constantly, he observed. The few times he did speak, his words hit dead center. The wise among us listened to those rare and precious words.

One practice, I was having a particularly difficult time

executing a turn for one of the strokes. I'd wade out to the flag, swim into the wall, and attempt the turn. Many, many tries later, I still wasn't getting it right. So I took a rest. Holding on to the wall, I was catching my breath and trying to figure out what was going wrong. My coach always had a kickboard in his hand, a constant tool. As I hung on the wall, I felt the (mostly gentle) thud of the kickboard on my head. He had my attention. I looked up at my coach through my swim goggles. Three words from my coach followed.

"You lack confidence."

Three words rolled around in my head: "You are right."

I have a friend who remembers hearing the same words from his dad. Over and over again, his dad told him he lacked confidence. On one occasion, my friend was going to ask a young lady out on a date. She said no. He told his dad about this. His dad was all poised to say something to him when the son interrupted and said, "I know, I know. You're going to say I lack confidence." The dad replied, "Well, I guess that is true too. But I was going to say you lack a car."

What we are really talking about here is not only a lack of confidence, but also a misplaced confidence. Or, to put it another way, we tend to put our confidence in the wrong thing and in the wrong place.

False confidence, or misplaced confidence, is a truly deadly thing.

Jerome might have had a misplaced confidence. Any Christian who lived after the year 312 might very well have been inclined to look favorably upon Rome. The horrors of persecution were mostly brought to an end with the legalization of Christianity in 312 by the Emperor Constantine.

The centuries of being marginalized economically, socially, and politically had been replaced with a new era of privilege and status for Christians. Constantine overturned 275 years of persecution. Jerome witnessed firsthand the benefits that had accrued since Constantine turned Rome's protection and Rome's power to Christians and not against them. In the 410s, that era of Roman glory and Christian triumph was coming to an end. The barbarians were at the gate.

Jerome was not sure of what was coming next. What would become of the world without Rome? What would become of Christianity without Rome? He traced out every possible scenario in his mind. It was all bleak. Jerome mistakenly placed his confidence in Rome and in the empire.

Boast in . . .

A similar occurrence happened in the life of Israel. The prophet Jeremiah had a front-row seat, prophesying the exile of God's people and then witnessing the exile and the harsh realities that came along with it. In his long prophetic book, he records the consequences of misplaced confidence. As a mouthpiece for God, he declares:

> Let not the wise man boast in his wisdom, let not the mighty man boast in his might, let not the rich man boast in his riches. (Jer. 9:23)

That takes care of about everything we naturally tend to put our confidence in. But then Jeremiah points us elsewhere:

> But let him who boasts, boast in this, that he understands and knows me, that I am the LORD who practices steadfast love, justice, and righteousness in the earth. For in these things I delight, declares the Lord. (Jer. 9:24)

Israel thought their hope and their future lay in acquiring wisdom, wealth, and might. Wisdom, wealth, and might are not necessarily bad things, either. In fact, Scripture in many places exhorts us to get wisdom. Abraham had great wealth, immense wealth. He was chastised for many things over the course of his life, but never for his wealth. Nations with wealth can use that for good. People can too. Nations, like Israel, must have might, must have power. Is strength a bad thing? It can be used for bad things, evil things. But is might to be categorically disdained and denied?

What does God want the Israelites to grasp on the eve of their exile? The answer is simple: the Israelites had missed the one thing they needed. Their future, their hope, and their success, rested in God alone. Nothing else. God was to be at the center. Their confidence was to be in God—not in their own wisdom, nor in their wealth, nor in their might.

We live in a momentous time. Through the technological advances of our age, information can be disseminated instantly. Change, even dramatic and substantive change, can occur rapidly. Consequently, the stakes are high. Change occurs rapidly, and it already has. There seems to be a seismic shift occurring.

We easily think of the changes occurring now as indicating that far worse things are to come. Like tremors before an earthquake, we all simply assume that the worse is yet to come.

We see these cultural shifts and capitulations and we instinctively know they only portend worse things yet. The world is coming to an end (again).

But this is not a time to cower, cave, or capitulate. It is a time for confidence, *and our confidence must be in the right place.* Or, better to say, our confidence must be in the right person. Our confidence must be in God. All else will disappoint.

It's the Object that Counts

Theologians remind us that we sometimes think wrongly of faith. We tend to think of faith in terms of degrees or intensity—*I need more faith.* This thinking especially manifests itself when we think of salvation. More faith, however, isn't the answer. My faith isn't the answer. The answer—in other words, what saves us—is the object of our faith.

I don't need to muster up more faith. I need to "up" the object of faith. I need to look to Christ. Want to live by faith? Look to Christ, learn of Christ, follow Christ, trust in Christ, and rest in Christ. The object makes all the difference.

So it is with confidence. The word *confidence* actually comes from the Latin word *fides*, meaning "faith." *Con-* is a prefix meaning "with." In this compound word, it functions as an intensive. "Full trust" is the idea behind the word *confidence*. Reliance, firmness—these are synonyms of the word *confidence*.

When we use the expression *lack of confidence*, what we are really talking about are distractions that get in the way of our confidence, of our reliance and full-throttle trust. Ultimately, fear kept me from making that turn in that pool. My coach knew that. He was telling me to have confidence in my training, to have confidence in his instruction, and to have confidence in my abilities.

Have you ever toed the line for a race? Taken your place at the starting block? Adrenaline pumping, nerves at full tilt? What do you need to do? Calm down. Remember your training. Have confidence.

What does the coach say in the locker room at halftime to the team that's down on the scoreboard? Do they run drills and watch films? Do they try to get in ten more minutes of training? Of course not. Instead, the inspiring speech comes. *You can do this*, assures the coach. *Calm down. Remember your training. Have confidence.*

Full faith, *intensive* faith. That's what confidence means.

As with athletes who are entering the arena, so it is with Christians in the arena of life. We need to have confidence. Unlike the athlete staring down the opponent, however, we are fools to put our confidence in ourselves. Athletes are supposed to put their confidence in their training. It's what they do. Christians, on the other hand, know that there's no sense whatsoever in putting any confidence in the flesh. Paul says clearly, "Put no confidence in the flesh" (Phil. 3:3).

We steadfastly and firmly rely upon our God. We have planted our flag with Him, in Him, and even through Him.

This moment in which we live is a time of change and confusion. But it cannot be a time of cowering or a time for hiding in a cave like Jerome. It is a time for confidence.

We looked at how Jerome responded to the collapse of Rome. Consider another early church father, Augustine, and his response to the collapse of Rome.

Augustine's great work *The Confessions* tells the story of the "Hound of Heaven" who tracked Augustine down. It tells the story of how God brought Augustine to Himself and brought him home. After his conversion, Augustine went on to be the bishop of Hippo Regius, an area of North Africa. Augustine, like Jerome, lived to witness the collapse of Rome in 410. From his deathbed twenty years later, Augustine coordinated the efforts of the city of Hippo as it tried in vain to withstand the siege of the Vandals. But what did Augustine do when the news of the beginning of Rome's collapse reached him? He went into his study and wrote what would come to be a classic. He wrote *The City of God*. It's a very long book, and early on, Augustine tells us, "This is a great work, this; it's arduous." By "great," he doesn't mean it's going to be excellent; he means it's going to be long, because he's going to tell the story of human history. Then he adds, "An arduous work, this, which raises us, not by a quite human arrogance, but by a divine grace, above all earthly dignities that totter on this shifting scene."[5] Do you hear that word he uses? He uses the word *totter*. Empires come and go. Nations come and go. Leaders come and go. Even our own abilities and achievements—all of it comes and goes.

This is the total opposite of Jerome. Jerome sees the

barbarians at the gate and says, "The world is in ruins! Yes!" Then he goes off into his cave. Augustine sees the same thing, but then he realizes what is the true and necessary perspective to have. He takes a transcendent perspective. Instead of focusing on what's happening on the horizon of the temporary, the temporal, and the earthly, Augustine looks up. Augustine knows that what happens on the earthly plane rests on shifting sands.

Augustine finishes his long book by turning our attention to the kingdom of God. The kingdom of God stands above all tottering kingdoms, empires, and nations. The kingdom of God is the final and ultimate reality. Augustine uses the perspective of the reality of the kingdom of God to help him understand the seismic change that was occurring and to help him navigate that change. So Augustine declares:

> How great shall be that happiness which shall be tainted with no evil, which shall lack no good, and which shall afford leisure for the praise of God who shall be all in all. There shall be the enjoyment of beauty. True honor shall be there. True peace shall be there. God Himself, who is the author of all virtue, shall be there and shall be its reward.[6]

Augustine could have this perspective on the collapse of the Roman Empire because he had placed his confidence in the right place. Jerome, on the other hand, had placed his confidence in the wrong place. He had his confidence in Caesar.

He had his confidence in Rome. When that wrong thing was shaken and crumbled, Jerome pulled a Chicken Little and went off into the cave.

In the chapters that follow, we will find the right place to put our confidence.

Chapter Two

CONFIDENCE
IN GOD

Behold, the nations are like a drop from a bucket.

—ISAIAH 40:15A

Everything that could go wrong did. The plague had come to his city. Their infant daughter died within a few short months of her birth. He had felt the pain of betrayal. He was still reeling from the throes of a war, with both sides feeling as if he had somehow let them down. He had started a movement that was nearly drowning him. This was one of the most difficult years of his life. The year was 1527, and Martin Luther wondered if he could survive it.

In the two years that led up to this dark year in his life, Luther had taken to hymn writing. As he was a lover of music as well as a lover of theology, hymns came naturally to him. In

1527, he wrote what has perhaps become the hymn of the Reformation, if not one of the most beloved hymns of all time.[1]

"Did we in our own strength confide?" Why in the world would we ever consider such a thing?

Luther knew the reality of human limitations. He was nearly omnicompetent, a driven individual. He was a larger-than-life personality. Yet, he knew his own limitations. In 1527, as stormy events surrounded him, he knew he needed to look beyond himself, past his own strength and ability. He knew that God alone is our "mighty fortress," our "bulwark never failing." He knew how futile it would be to trust in our own strength.

The point of this entire book is captured in this one hymn from Martin Luther. Luther based the hymn on Psalm 46, which thunders, "The God of Jacob is our fortress." That phrase is not abstract; it is richly textured. This is the God of Jacob. We know of the foibles of Jacob. We also know of God's tender and never-ending care of Jacob. This is a God who sees, hears, knows, and cares. This is not a far-off, aloof God. This God who cared for Jacob is our fortress. This phrase from Psalm 46 prompted Luther to think of all the benefits that belong to us.

What do we have? We have the Spirit, and we have the gifts. They are ours; they belong to us.

Who is on our side? "The Man of God's own choosing." Christ, our elder brother, our Lord and Redeemer, He is on our side. "Christ Jesus, it is he," are the reassuring words that flow from Luther's pen. Christ fights for us against all our foes.

Should we have confidence in the outcome of this fight? The answer is clear: "He will win the battle."

What abides? "God's Word abideth still." In another hymn, Luther declares: "I'll trust in God's unchanging Word." It alone stands. God's Word alone abides.

And what about us? Well, "the body they may kill." Is that true? Is that existentially true? There is only one way in which this could be true. It is true only if God is our fortress and if "God's truth abideth still." This is not simply hyperbole. Luther was prone to extreme language, but he meant every word of this line.

The last line of Luther's hymn tells what ultimately matters: "His Kingdom is forever."

That is the resounding truth that anchored Luther in the storms of 1527. It is God. It is His Son. It is His Word. It is His Spirit. It is His Kingdom. This is what matters.

And here is the singular truth that abides. It's the same truth that Augustine used as his anchor when Rome collapsed around him. God's kingdom is forever. That's the reality. The God of Jacob proves Himself to be a mighty fortress century after century.

What about the Storms, What about the Battle?

Luther's "A Mighty Fortress Is Our God" is an inspiring hymn. I vividly remember singing this hymn at the opening of the Philadelphia Conference on Reformed Theology in 1993. The historic Tenth Presbyterian Church, in the nicely appointed Rittenhouse Square area of one of America's fabled cities, played host. The church's magnificent pipe organ led the congregation.

The windows were open, and on that cool spring evening, the streets of Philadelphia were filled with the words of Martin Luther's hymn. As I bring the moment back in my mind's eye, I still get chills.

But that's at a conference with more than a thousand kindred spirits with hearts and minds and voices knit together in worship and awe of God. How does all this translate in the true storms of life? And what do we do about all of our enemies at the gate who are ready to bring us down?

Let's identify these enemies. From the beginning, they have been three: the world, the flesh, and the devil. Through the centuries, they have transformed and have taken on the trappings of the age, but their base nature remains the same. They stand in opposition to God, His people, and His kingdom. They conspire together—and the sum is greater than the parts.

One of the most comforting texts in the Old Testament is Isaiah 40. It is a text of intense beauty. From the first verse to the last, the text is sheer poetry. It is also sheer theology. This text even played a role in one of the twentieth century's great movies, *Chariots of Fire*, the story of Scottish Olympian and then missionary to China Eric Liddell.[2]

On the eve of the Olympics, Liddell faced immense political pressure, even from a prince. Yet, he did not back down. Liddell, a clear favorite for the 100 meters, could not run that event in the 1924 Paris Olympics. The first heat for the 100 was scheduled on a Sunday. His Scottish Presbyterian convictions would not allow him to run on the Sabbath. But Great Britain needed him. The Prince of Wales, among his many ceremonial duties, served as titular head of the British Olympic Committee. He was brought in to convince Liddell to run. Liddell stood his ground.

Instead, Liddell focused his attention on the 200 meters and began training for the 400 meters, an entirely new event for him. The 400 meters is considered a middle-distance run, not a sprinting event like the 100 and the 200. At the world-class level of competition, sprinters don't make good middle-distance runners.

Liddell took the respectable bronze in the 200 meters. He shocked the world, however, when he won gold in the 400. He was hailed as a champion's champion.

On the Sunday he would have been running in that 100-meter opening heat, he instead preached in a church. His text was Isaiah 40, a fitting text given the reference to running in verse 31. It's also fitting due to the references to the nations throughout the chapter. What are the nations? They are but drops in the bucket.

Other enemies lurk in these verses in Isaiah 40. There are the idols and false gods, the false religions in Israel's day and of Israel's neighbors. There are the mighty forces of nature against which we have to contend. Last, add our own frailties, weaknesses, and feeble flesh. The enemies stack up in this chapter.

God is there at every turn. We need to learn this lesson from Isaiah 40 anew today.

Comfort, Comfort My People

Isaiah 40 serves as a turning point in the book of Isaiah. The previous thirty-nine chapters have largely consisted of one long, relentless speech after another—speeches of judgment, mayhem, and destruction. By the time you are finished with chapter 39, you are feeling rather bleak, rather beaten down. Israel, the nations, and virtually all people on the earth come under the storm cloud of God's judgment. Sin was the seed that had been sown. The harvest of judgment was coming.[3]

Then we look at chapter 40, verse 1. A remarkable word jumps off the page—twice! "Comfort, comfort my people, says your God." Like a cascading waterfall in a parched land, the verses of chapter 40 flow over us, refreshing and comforting. At the center of this refreshment and comfort stands but one thing. God and His salvation towers over all enemies, obstacles, and hindrances. He is our God, and He will deliver us.

In chapter 40, Isaiah is prophesying to a group of people, God's chosen nation, who were exiled in a strange land. Their homeland, the Promised Land, had been besieged and laid waste. The formerly holy city of Jerusalem was a pile of rubble. The temple lay in ruins. Isaiah 40:1–11 prophesies Israel's return to the land. God, the faithful and good shepherd, would scoop up His little lambs in His arms, hold them against His bosom, and carry them safely back to their land, back to their home.

This message of comfort aims directly at those people in exile. In your mind's eye, picture them around a campfire in that foreign land. Huddled together, these exiles are trying to make sense of what has happened to them. They were God's chosen nation and now they are squarely under the thumb of a foreign ruler. And God promised to lead them safely home.

How difficult would it be to receive that promise? If you

were looking at the circumstances, seeing the temporal, would you be quick to believe? Or would you have your doubts?

We need to explore this a little further. Israel had not been taken captive by just any ruler or just any kingdom. They were defeated and carried off by the great Nebuchadnezzar and the Babylonian Empire. Babylon was the greatest empire the world had seen—until the next one. The Babylonian Empire was succeeded by the Medo-Persian Empire, which became the next world superpower. The legendary Cyrus ruled the Medo-Persians. He ruled over the captured people of Israel. They were the chattel of this ancient tyrant.

Cyrus came to the throne in 539 BC. At the time, he ruled over a small area of modern-day southeastern Iran. That same year, he successfully invaded Babylon. Over the next nine years, he created the largest empire ever seen up to that point in human history. Among his many titles was King of the Four Corners of the World.

In 539 BC, he decreed that Israel would be allowed to return to their land; they would be allowed to rebuild their city Jerusalem and rebuild their temple. This is recorded in 2 Chronicles 36:22 and in Ezra 6:3–5. It was also prophesied by Isaiah in Isaiah 45:1–6. Isaiah speaks of Cyrus—names him—as the human instrument anointed by God to return Israel to their Promised Land. Isaiah speaks of Cyrus by name more than one hundred years before Cyrus even began to rule.

Of course, the biblical account has been called into question by critics and skeptics. That prophecy of Cyrus in Isaiah 45 has even led these critics to posit two "Isaiahs," that is, two sections of the book of Isaiah with two different authors. The first Isaiah wrote chapters 1–39. The second Isaiah did not write a prophecy, but a history. So the "second author" wrote chapters 40–66 as a history of the return from exile.

Part of the critics' argument is the lack of any extrabiblical corroboration of Cyrus' decree to allow the exiles to return. Why would Cyrus, the King of the Four Corners of the World, concern himself with the plight of a rather inconsequential group of people?

Then, in 1879, archaeologists discovered the Cyrus Cylinder in the temple of Marduk in Babylon. It contains the declaration of Cyrus that decreed the return of the Israelites to their land. History, exactly as the Bible has it.

There is no solid ground to argue for two Isaiahs. The main argument simply opposes the implication of a single author. If Isaiah's prophecy is true, does that not support the fact that the Bible is not merely a human book by a human author?

Beyond the issue of answering critics, we need to look to Isaiah 40 for what it teaches about placing our confidence in God.

Isaiah was writing a prophecy. It was intended for a captive and exiled people to trust in God's promises and to trust in Him to deliver them. Isaiah 40:1–11 is one long declaration of a glorious promise of redemption.

God will make a way. He will straighten paths, remove mountains, and fill in the lowlands (Isa. 40:3–4). There will be no uneven ground, no rough places to keep these exiles from making their way back to the Promised Land. Far more, all of this serves only as the backdrop for the revelation of the glory of God, as Isaiah 40:5 declares: "And the glory of the LORD shall be revealed, and all flesh shall see it together."

The Lord had spoken. Israel was then to be a prophetic voice to the nations declaring the greatness of God. In verse 9, the prophet is to get up on a high mountain and herald.

What do heralds do? They herald. They shout and proclaim. This particular herald was given a particular task: to proclaim the "good news" of God's redemption and deliverance. He was to point to the inhabitants of the cities of Judah. Once he had their attention, he was to lift their eyes off of the temporary and temporal and on to the transcendent. This herald pointed people to God.

"Behold your God!" declares the prophet. *Behold* is the right word. We tend to use the word *behold* sparingly. It is a word reserved for an impressive thing or impressive person. This is not a mere look. This is not a furtive glance. *Behold* means to really see.

So the prophet says, "Behold your God!" And we look intently and intensely at our God, our impressive God. What do we see as we look?

In chapters 1–39, we see the whirlwind of judgment, thunderbolts clapping, lightning flashing. This is the God we behold. Now, consider this picture from Isaiah 40:10–11:

> Behold, the Lord GOD comes with might,
>   and his arm rules for him;
> behold, his reward is with him,
>   and his recompense before him.

He will tend his flock like a shepherd;
    he will gather the lambs in his arms;
he will carry them in his bosom,
    and gently lead those that are with young.

This is a tender picture of the mighty God stooping low to gather us into His arms, to lift us up and to carry us close, to carry us all the way to His perfect plan of redemption. We see here a picture of the tender mercies of God.

Consider, though, for a moment the perspective of these captive and exiled people who heard this as they sat around the campfires in Babylon and longed for this deliverance. They were told to behold their God, but all they could see was Babylon. All they saw was Nebuchadnezzar and Cyrus. They only saw obstacles. Defeated people have difficulty seeing past the defeat.

How hard would it be to see God's promises of deliverance through the ever-present armies of Nebuchadnezzar and Cyrus? How hard would it be to accept that these powerful and mighty kings were not truly in control, but that God was in control—all appearances to the contrary?

If we were in exile, far from home, would we have our doubts? Would we have full confidence in what God promises in Isaiah 40:1–11? I suspect that in the honest moments, these promises of deliverance would be met with doubt. "Let's be realistic about our situation," one would be tempted to say. "Why get our hopes up when they most certainly will only be dashed?"

What follows in verses 12–31 answers all doubts and crushes

all hesitations and suspicions. In these verses, the prophet launches into a series of demonstrations of God's power to bring His promise to fruition.

God declares deliverance in verses 1–11. God demonstrates his power to deliver in verses 12–31. Matthew Henry wrote of Isaiah 40:12–31 that "the scope of these verses is to show what a great and glorious Being the Lord Jehovah is."[4]

In verses 12–31 of Isaiah 40, we are shown the power and the greatness of what God can do so that we can behold the glory and greatness of who God is.

These demonstrations of God's power start with creation and the great power of nature. In verse 12, we have seas, the expanse of the heavens, the earth itself, and mountains. All of these put us in our place. Have you ever stood before the ocean waves? Watch kids as they play on the beach. In rolls the wave and they go upended. Wave after relentless wave. And what of a storm on an ocean? Or even a lake? What of the power of a rushing river? The force of water from a waterfall?

When you look up into the night's sky, as the immense stars come into focus, do you ever feel small?

And what of this globe we live on? We have circumnavigated it, but who are we in light of it?

Then there are the mountains. Perhaps nothing reminds us of our frailty and smallness like a mountain. We build skyscrapers. We fly at 36,000 feet. But to stand before a snow-capped peak takes our breath away.

Seas, skies, earth, and mountains—all beautiful and glorious and yet foreboding and terrifying at the same time. As great as these things are, they are nothing compared to God. He holds the waters in the hollow of His hand, these seas that terrified ancient mariners. God weighs these mountains in scales. Seas and mountains, the universe—they are all transcendent things to our human experience, capability, and even our existence. Yet God transcends them all further still. God is more powerful than creation, than the great and terrifying forces of nature.

Next, the prophet appears to move from discussing God's omnipotence, His being all-powerful, to His omniscience, His knowing all. The topic, however, is still God's omnipotence in Isaiah 40:13–14. This time, God demonstrates His power over the false gods and idols.

In the Babylonian pantheon of gods, Marduk was the chief god, like Zeus for the Greeks or Ra, the sun god, for the Egyptians. Yet Marduk was not the only god. There were other gods. In the Babylonian understanding, Marduk would hold counsel by gathering the other gods together. He would consult with them, using their particular expertise before deciding what course of action to take. As a president consults with his cabinet, so Marduk took counsel.

Now consider God:

> Whom did he consult,
>   and who made him understand?
> Who taught him the path of justice,
>   and taught him knowledge,
>   and showed him the way of understanding? (v. 14)

These are all rhetorical questions, and they all are met with a resounding answer: no one. This is a clear declaration of the supremacy of God over the so-called gods. God is more powerful than the false gods, idols, and religious systems.

In the ancient world, the common religious understanding held that if one nation defeated another nation, then that meant the superiority of the victorious nation's gods over the gods of the conquered nation. This was not a secular culture with a secular worldview. It was a deeply religious culture. To be sure, the religion was fatally flawed, but it was nevertheless religious to the core. When Babylon conquered Israel, did that mean Babylon's gods were superior? Did Marduk beat Yahweh?

Earlier in Isaiah, the prophet is quick to point out a different dynamic at work in Israel. Israel's defeat signaled nothing even akin to the weakness of Yahweh. Instead, God stayed His protective hand so that Babylon would be His instrument in bringing judgment on His people. Why did God judge Israel? They had broken covenant. God had promised that if they kept the covenant, He would bless them in the land and prosper their hand. If they broke covenant, they would incur the covenant curses. They would feel the hand of judgment. God did not fail Israel. God did not waver. Israel disobeyed and rebelled.

There are many Hebrew words for sin. One is *pasha*, which means "covenant rebellion." It was used of nations when they broke a treaty with another nation. They would *pasha*; they would rebel.

In the second verse of the book of Isaiah, we bump into this word. Israel rebelled against God (Isa. 1:2). God did not sleep;

God did not blink. Israel failed to keep covenant. Consequently, Israel felt the harsh realities of judgment and exile.

Nevertheless, the question still lingered in the minds of the captive and exiled Israelites: *Is God strong enough to deliver us from the clutches of these Babylonian gods?* The answer was a resounding yes, because God is the supreme God.

Isaiah 40 turns next to the nations, those that collectively form but a drop in the bucket. Lebanon was known for its vast forests of cedar, quite a commodity in itself. Those vast cedar forests yielded yet another resource: the animals that lived there. Yet all that cedar and all of those animals would not combine to make one scintilla of the amount necessary for the sacrifice (v. 16).

All of the nations have a sum total of nothingness. In fact, they are less than nothing (v. 17). Psalm 2 asks why the nations, in futility, rage? They flex their muscles. They roar. But all to no avail. World rulers froth and foam. But it is all babble.

Nebuchadnezzar himself becomes exhibit A. This great ruler, possessing wealth and power unprecedented in his day, found himself reduced to madness.

We cower before despots and leaders. The twentieth century witnessed a full complement of tyrants, true megalomaniacs, who committed atrocities and genocide. In the twenty-first century, thugs serve as heads of state and rogue leaders relentlessly threaten and carry out violence. So we need to hear these words: "All the nations are as nothing before him." We need to be reminded of God's power over the nations.

Here especially, we need vision over sight, as mentioned in

chapter one. If all we do is see what is front of us, only see what is right on our horizon, we will easily despair. We can easily doubt. So we must have vision. We must have the vision of God, our all in all.

In the second century, Polycarp, bishop of Smyrna, was martyred. He wrote a chronicle of his arrest and imprisonment. His associates finished the account, recording his death. It is a fascinating text. In the early church, it was very popular. It was circulated alongside of the New Testament Epistles and was widely read. The Epistle of Polycarp was intended to encourage other Christians as they faced or would come to face persecution. Polycarp's example of an unwavering commitment to God, no matter the cost, inspired and encouraged many in the second century, and it has continued to do so even right down to our own time.

One of the most encouraging lines is this: "Polycarp was taken prisoner by Herod, when Philip the Trallian was High Priest, when Statius Quadratus was proconsul, and when Jesus Christ is king forever, to whom be glory, honor, majesty, and an everlasting throne, from generation to generation."[5]

This line assured the Christians who faced persecution in those early centuries that Rome was not in charge. Caesars and proconsuls, high priests and mid-level bureaucrats appear to be in charge, but they are not. Jesus Christ rules. He alone is King.

This was the lesson for second-century Christians in Rome. It was the lesson for Israel while it was under the thumb of Babylon and Medo-Persia. It is the lesson for us today. It is probably one of the easiest lessons for us to learn academically. Anyone who can read and who will submit to God's Word will conclude that God is in control. They will mentally affirm that and assent to that. To know this doctrine experientially might be another thing altogether. Knowing it experientially means to trust and not to fear. Knowing it experientially means to boldly proclaim and live by the gospel and not to cower and cave and give up those beliefs in light of opposition and challenge.

The body they may kill? Easier to sing than to live.

At this point in Isaiah 40, the prophet stops to take stock. God's power has been demonstrated over creation, over the false gods, and over the nations. So, the prophet offers us a rhetorical question to remind us that God is unrivaled: "To whom then will you liken God?" (v. 16).

Immediately, we start into another cycle of demonstrations of God's power. Again, we're back to idols and false gods. Here we have some delightful sarcasm. Some idols are cast and overlaid in gold. But for those of lesser means, wood suffices. Buyer beware, however. Make sure you employ a skilled craftsman. If you don't, the wooden idol will wobble and will fall down (v. 21).

It would be centuries before human beings would soar at 36,000 feet, allowing all those things on the ground to appear so tiny. God has had a far higher perspective all along. As armies move and empires build and stretch, they all appear as insects to God (v. 22). The vast heavens are merely God's tent. God, again, dominates nature. And, again, the power of God dominates the princes and the nations as God brings them to nothing. They are like a disappearing vapor (v. 23).

The case has been made. God's power has been demonstrated

vividly, continuously, and forcefully from verse 12 all the way through verse 26.

Yet doubt still remains. Notice verse 27: "Why do you say, O Jacob, and speak, O Israel, 'My way is hidden from the LORD, and my right is disregarded by my God?'" The prophet anticipates the doubt, the suspicion. It's one thing for these grand, even abstract, statements regarding God's power, but does God notice me? Will His omnipotence reach down to my present moment, my challenge, my fear, and my doubt?

First, consider that this question is even recorded. That is telling. We live in what many have called the "already/not yet." Our redemption is already and not yet accomplished. The kingdom is already and not yet here. Sometimes we experience very little of the already. So much seems not yet. It is hard to live in between the promise and the fulfillment of that promise. It is easy to ask, *Does God notice me?* We never admit that we ask such questions, and we rarely verbalize such questions. Yet, we do ask them.

It is also easy to be perplexed at the seeming triumph of evil. To quote the blues singer Son House, "I know there will be justice in the eternal by and by, but what about a little justice here and now?" We can ask either in despair or in utter desire to stop seeing evil triumph and righteousness punished. That Scripture records this question is encouraging. That God has an answer is far more encouraging still.

John Calvin sees dejection, despondency, and utter despair all packed into this question. Calvin also sees this: "The Lord intends to stir the hearts of the Godly, that they might not faint, amidst heavy calamities . . . that they might not sink under any distresses however long and continued."[6]

Does God notice me? still remains as the question. To answer it, Isaiah brings one final demonstration of God's power. Like a good storyteller, he has saved the best for last. The final demonstration of God's power is this: God demonstrates His power in the lives of His people. Ultimately, God not only demonstrates His power, but He delights to do so, in the lives of His people. This is our confidence in God: He delights to save us, to help us, to keep us, to strengthen us, and to comfort us.

In our desperate state, when we have reached our limits, we are ready to see the one thing we should have been focused on all along. Matthew Henry wisely put it this way: "We must, therefore, be fully convinced of our weakness that we may yield to the power of God."

At the end of Isaiah 40, we see our weakness on bold display. We also see God's strength bolder still. Meditate upon these words:

Have you not known? Have you not heard?
The LORD is the everlasting God,
    the Creator of the ends of the earth.
He does not faint or grow weary;
    his understanding is unsearchable.
He gives power to the faint,
    and to him who has no might he increases strength.
Even youths shall faint and be weary,
    and young men shall fall exhausted;

> but they who wait for the LORD shall renew their strength;
>   they shall mount up with wings like eagles;
> they shall run and not be weary;
>   they shall walk and not faint. (vv. 28–31)

God's strength stands in clear contrast to human weakness. Take the symbol of human energy: youths. Every parent knows that all you have to do is wait them out. They will burst in moments of astounding energy. But they, even the most energetic of them, have limits. Or, take the symbol of strength and vigor: young men. They, too, have limits, and will reach them.

Javier Sotomayor set the world record for the high jump at an impressive 8 feet, ¼ inches. That was in 1993. I'm not sure how high he's jumping these days, but I'm very certain he's not surpassing eight feet. At some point, we reach the end of ourselves. We admit with Luther and his hymn that our striving would be losing. Gently, the prophet tells us to wait on God. The Lord renews our strength.

There was a particular application of these verses to the original audience of Isaiah. The promise of return to the Promised Land not only meant being freed from the grip of the tyrant Cyrus, it also included the journey to get there. There was no easy way to get from the cities of Babylon to Jerusalem in the fifth century BC. The journey for individuals, or even for a family or clan, came with challenges enough. Imagine the task of moving a people group back, a people including infants and toddlers and the very old, the weak and the challenged. Even the young men, who can break records in the high jump and seem to have an unending cache of energy—all who made this journey would faint. Every last one would reach their limit and fall in exhaustion. But those who waited on God, He would strengthen and enable. When the prophet says "wait" here—and he uses the word many times in the book—he calls us to pause, to stop relying on ourselves or on our plans or schemes. Waiting means to move out of the way and to wholly trust and rely upon God.

Those who do wait upon the Lord are promised that God will renew their strength. The prophet highlights and expands this overarching promise with three metaphors in verse 31. Isaiah uses three specific illustrations to demonstrate how fully and how certainly God's strength renews us. These three illustrations drive home the point of God's power.

Initially, we might think the order of these three illustrations should be reversed. The order seems anticlimactic. We'd rather fly like an eagle than run, and we certainly would rather soar through the air than walk. Yet, Isaiah uses walking as the culminating illustration. As we reflect on this, however, we see how the order is entirely spot on.

The soaring like an eagle, running, and walking are all metaphors. Let's carry the metaphor through. Seldom do we need those bursts of strength to fly like an eagle, and occasionally we need to run, but consistently and constantly we walk. It's rather mundane. You might even use the word *ordinary*. And so, it is in the ordinary that God meets us. God meets us at our everyday tasks and at the momentous occasions of our life, and everywhere in between. There is nothing we do that is too little, nor is there anything we do that is too big, for God to work in us and for God to strengthen us. It is in the activities of our lives and the events of our lives that God shows Himself and proves Himself able. In all the moments and activities of our lives, God is demonstrating His power in us and through us.

God delights to demonstrate His power in the lives of His people. As they live in between the promise and its fulfillment, they wait; they find their power in God. So we can be confident. Is our situation as bad as Israel's was, as they sat beside a campfire under a foreign oppressor with deliverance generations away?

Yet, Isaiah's audience was commanded to look to God, to be confident in God. God would pick them up like little lambs and bring them home. This is a word of comfort. God alone is worthy of our confidence. It is we who miss out when we fail to put our confidence in God. Luther was right: "A mighty fortress is our God, a bulwark never failing."

R.C. Sproul has said many times that our biggest problem is that we don't know who God is and we don't know who we are. Isaiah 40 is a good place to start to learn about God and about ourselves. We have only scratched the surface of who God is in chapter 40 of the book of Isaiah. He is omnipotent, omniscient, omnibenevolent. He is holy, just, good, righteous, and pure. He is full of mercy and compassion, long-suffering, gracious, and most kind. He is our God.

Isaiah is also a good place to learn about Christ. Ultimately, the deliverance that Isaiah poetically describes in chapter 40 owes everything to Him. It is all because of Christ. One of the hardest phrases in all of Scripture comes a few chapters after

Isaiah 40 in 53:10. Do you know why God ultimately fulfills His promise and demonstrates His power? It is because of our elder brother, Christ. Do you know why it is we can walk and not faint? Do you know why we can run and not grow weary? How we can soar like an eagle? There was a time when Christ could not walk, and He fainted under the power of His cross. He took upon Himself our sin and our unrighteousness, our weakness, our frailty, our inability. Do you feel the weight of Isaiah 53:10? Hear these devastating words: "Yet it was the will of the LORD to crush him."

As we think of these beautiful verses of Isaiah 40, we know these are true because of those horrific verses in Isaiah 53. There is One who did faint for us. There is One who was crushed for us. And God, in power, raised Him from the dead.

The ultimate demonstration of the power of God is at the cross and at the empty tomb. Because of that demonstration of God's power at the cross and at the resurrection, we are His people, we are His lambs. God will gather us up in His arms. This is our God. In Him we firmly and securely put our confidence. God will never disappoint. For He tells us:

Fear not, for I am with you;
> be not dismayed, for I am your God;
I will strengthen you, I will help you,
> I will uphold you with my righteous right hand.
> (Isa. 41:10)

Chapter Three

CONFIDENCE
IN THE BIBLE

I'll trust in God's unchanging word
till soul and body sever,
for, though all things shall pass away,
His Word shall stand forever.

—Martin Luther

The wisdom of God was not given for any particular age,
but for all ages. It surely therefore becomes us to receive
what God reveals to be truth and to look upon His Word.

—Jonathan Edwards

I n a *New York Times* op-ed on April 3, 2015, Frank Bruni sounded off on "Bigotry, the Bible and the Lessons of Indiana," referencing the drama that accompanied the passing of Indiana's Religious Freedom Restoration Act. Bruni contended that to take a position that condemns certain lifestyles and sexual orientations "prioritizes scattered passages of ancient texts over all that has been learned since—as if time had stood still, as if the advances of science and knowledge meant nothing."

Bruni continued his attempt to make the case that we now know so much better than the ancients, so much better than the biblical authors. Again, the position that would condemn certain sexual orientations "elevates unthinking obeisance above intelligent observance, above the evidence in front of you, because to look honestly at gay, lesbian and bisexual people is to see that we're the same magnificent riddles as everyone else: no more or less flawed, no more or less dignified."

Discard the Bible. It no longer makes sense of our world or of our existence.

This is a direct assault on the Bible. And Bruni is not alone. A culture that thinks it knows better than the Bible surrounds us. Many loud voices have chimed in to call for giving up altogether on this ancient book that is so out of step with life in the twenty-first century.

The Golden Globe–winning series *Transparent*, launched in 2014 by Amazon Studios, presents the mainstreaming of gender transformation. The family of the main character realizes their dad was not always a dad. The show itself represents the phenomenon of art imitating reality. Jill Soloway, the show's creator and producer, has a transgender father. She used a "transformative action program" in hiring for the show, giving preference to transgender individuals. All of the bathrooms on set are transgender.

In the very first chapter of the very first book of the Bible, we read these words: "Male and female he created them" (Gen. 1:27c).

The transgender revolution is in fact not a revolution but a rebellion, a rebellion against the very clear teaching of Scripture—and the very nature of the universe. Gender is not a construct. It is a reality.

While these particular attacks are new, attacks on the Bible are nothing new. At the beginning of the twentieth century, the challenge came from the sciences. Charles Darwin's view of origins ruled. His view first started washing ashore in the United States in the late 1800s. Old Testament scholars thought Darwin offered a better explanation of the universe than the opening chapters of Genesis did. Darwinism spread quickly. By 1925, the year of the famous Scopes Trial, Darwinism had won out among the cultural elites in America. The Scopes Trial pitted the state of Tennessee against John Thomas Scopes, a junior high science teacher who used a textbook that referred to evolution. The state of Tennessee had the law on its side. Teaching evolution was prohibited by an act of the Tennessee General Assembly called the Butler Act. The case garnered media attention and was soon dubbed the "Trial of the Century"—though there would come to be many more trials so designated. All eyes were on the courtroom in Dayton, Tennessee. The issue had far more to do with the case at hand. Clarence Darrow, attorney for the defense, put the Bible on trial.

The issue in that Tennessee courtroom was the crucial question of the twentieth century. Does God's Word still hold true? Does the Bible matter? To put the question more person-ally, are we going to listen to a book that's two thousand to five thousand years old, or are we going to pay attention to modern science? That was the issue. It was really that simple. To be for evolution was to be urban, current, informed, and cultured. To adhere to Genesis 1 was to be uninformed and uncultured, a country bumpkin who lived in the far and distant past.

There was another front to the attack on the Bible at the dawn of the twentieth century. If Darwin and evolution came from without, this attack came from within, from the religious establishment. In the 1910s, Billy Sunday, the former profes-sional baseball player turned fiery evangelist, held massive crusades across America's cities. He was known for his acrobatic preaching. In fact, in some moments, Sunday could even leap from the platform to the top of the pulpit. He would get right up on the edge of the platform and he would thunder, "Turn hell upside down, and you know what's stamped on the bottom? Made in Germany!" It was the time of World War I, and the world was arrayed against Germany. But that's not entirely what Sunday meant. What Sunday meant was higher criticism.

Higher criticism came from English and German scholars, but the German scholars of the nineteenth century receive all of the attention. First, higher critics examined and scrutinized the Pentateuch, challenging Mosaic authorship. When they fin-ished their critical, historical, and philological investigations, they reached the conclusion that the Pentateuch expressed man's sense of the divine. It was not a divinely inspired word from God to man. Higher critics of the Old Testament identified four authorial strands in the first five books of the Bible, which were formerly attributed to Moses under the inspiration of the Holy Spirit. Higher critics also turned to examine Isaiah and again discovered a different account than was previously held. Isaiah, too, was the work of human authors alone, expressing their encounter with and their sense of the divine. These scholars concluded that Isaiah is history, not prophecy.

Then came time to examine the Gospels. This began what is known as the "quest for the historical Jesus." There are two Jesuses in the final form of the four Gospels, according to this quest. One is the Jesus of faith, who is the embellished Jesus. He is the Jesus of the faith communities that rose up after the first century. The other is the Jesus of history, the Jesus that actually existed. So the scholars in this quest seek the kernel of truth amid all the trappings of myth and embellishment.

You can follow this thread of higher criticism all through the twentieth century and even down to our own day. The Jesus Seminar produced *The Five Gospels* (the fifth being the Gospel of Thomas), and figures such as Bart Ehrman and Elaine Pagels have written numerous books and appear regularly on media outlets explaining how the New Testament *really* came about. Ehrman, Pagels, and others write the textbooks on the Bible that are used in freshman religious classes across college and university campuses.

In our day, attacks continue from the sciences. These have been joined with volleys from the social sciences. The gurus on human identity and human nature—sociologists, cultural anthropologists, and culture studies experts—line up to tell us how best to think of ourselves, our identity, and our sexuality.

Jill Soloway had her first epiphany regarding transgender issues in a culture studies class while an undergrad at the University of Wisconsin–Madison. Ideas have consequences. Bad ideas have bad consequences.

At the turn of the twentieth century, the sciences supposedly knew better than the Bible. Now, the social sciences supposedly know better than the Bible. And we are seeing this new world-view presented artfully and entertainingly through a barrage of media and in the halls of the academy. A casual watcher and listener will be exposed to countless gay, bisexual, and transgender individuals, acts, and ideas—and all without ever leaving mainstream media outlets. These are the times we live in (see TheStateofTheology.com).

These challenges have a cumulative effect. They become self-fulfilling prophecies. The promoters and producers of this material not only want to make room for these biblically aberrant views, they want to increase the tribe. They want to silence anyone who would stand up against them. They want to oppose anyone who would say, "What you are promoting and doing is wrong."

The proverbial silver lining in these challenges to the Bible in our day is that they bring a great deal of clarity to the issue before us as Christians: Will our authority be the Word of God? Or will it be the sensibilities of our age? Is it the Bible? Or is it us?[1]

These new challenges actually raise three questions we must consider. The first concerns how this affects us personally. Are we subtly influenced by all of this moral decay? To ask this another way: Have we moved the line because culture is trying to erase the line?

The second question concerns us as a larger entity, as the body of Christ. Will we continue to hold to our biblical convictions in the face of increasing pressure and possible persecution? Beware of the leader who wants to "rethink" what the Bible says or how we apply the Bible to these current situations and contexts. We must reaffirm the truth of the past. We must reaffirm orthodox and historic theology and biblical understanding. But we must never rethink the Bible's teaching. We would much prefer, for instance, that our boss reaffirm the decision to hire us rather than rethink it. The language of rethinking or accommodating should set off alarm bells in our heads. When you hear those bells go off, run.

On the other hand, we must show solidarity with those leaders who stand for biblical convictions. We must show solidarity with churches that stand for biblical convictions. This is a time for boundaries. Boundaries help us know who is not with us. But boundaries also help us know who is with us. And we need each other, perhaps now more than ever before. We need to encourage those who take strong stands on biblical convictions. Those who do take such strong stands get criticized, and that criticism can be sharp and cutting. Part of the beauty of the body of Christ is our care for one another, our encouragement for one another. As the surrounding culture turns more hostile, that mutual encouragement moves from being a luxury to a necessity.

The third question concerns our duties as a citizen, and as an ambassador of the truth and the gospel in this strange and foreign world. As Christians, we hold ourselves to biblical convictions and each other to biblical convictions. How do we, however, stand up for biblical convictions in the marketplace?

We must let the Bible be our guide. If it's a gospel issue, then we must take our stand. If it's a biblical truth matter, then we must take our stand. God has spoken on the nature of human identity and sexual identity. God has spoken on marriage.

All three of these lines in the sand are drawn in the opening two chapters of the Bible. God makes it clear that He created us, that He created male and female, and that He designed marriage to be between a man and a woman. Those three foundational truths are clear. All three are rejected today.

How that message will be received is of no consequence. Remember Luther's hymn? "The body they may kill." Our calling is to be faithful witnesses to God's revealed will. We cannot allow unhappy and undesirable consequences to keep us from obedience to that calling.

Again, the challenges of our day bring a new level of clarity to our calling and to our commitment. They drive us back to the Word of God with an increased urgency to listen. The assault on God's Word drives us right back to that same Word. These assaults do not weaken our faith in God's Word. Instead, these assaults force us to put our confidence in it.

The Bible Really Is God's Word

Of course, we can go back long before our day, long before Jill Soloway, before the Jesus Seminar, before Darwin and the Scopes Trial, to see assaults on the authority of God's Word. To find the first challenge, we need to go pretty far back, all the way back to the beginning. The garden of Eden provides the setting for the first assault, launched by the serpent, then by Eve, and then by Adam. The descendants of the first couple have continued the family tradition.

There is nothing new to challenges to God's Word.[2]

Paul knew of challenges to God's Word. In order to steel his young churches and their congregants, he reminded them of what they were reading when they read the Bible. In 1 Thessalonians 2:13, Paul offers one of the most succinct statements on the doctrine of Scripture. Paul loved the Thessalonian church. He had some issues with some of the churches that he had planted. (The church at Corinth comes to mind on that score.) But, when you read his epistles to the Thessalonians, you get a sense of the genuine, mutual love that Paul and the church at Thessalonica had for each other. He likens his time with them to a father's being with his children. Paul gave his very life to the believers in Thessalonica for the establishment of the church. When Paul remembers his time there, fond memories flood back.

Then, in 1 Thessalonians 2:13, Paul says, "And we also thank God constantly for this, that when you received the word of God, which you heard from us. . . ." Let's pause right there. Paul proclaimed the Word of God. This was his job. All of us have the same job. We have vocations, and we have things we do, but our main job is to proclaim the Word of God.

So Paul continues, "When you received the word of God, which you heard from us, you accepted it not as the word of men. . . ." In the first century, there were a lot of words of men.

The Greco-Roman world was rife with philosophers who peddled their philosophies. They would hustle into town with their oratorical skill and would set up on the porch in the public square, and they would wow the crowd with a new idea or some new application of an idea. There were plenty of "words of men" in Paul's day. These were the Romans with their Greek heritage. They had Socrates, Plato, and Aristotle. They had Homer, Herodotus, and Seneca. They had Euclid and Archimedes. They loved novel ideas, new systems of thought. They debated. They shot down the old ideas. They were always looking to the promise of something new. They prized philosophers, poets, scientists, and playwrights. They reveled in the words of men.

Paul says his message is not that. The Bible is not the words of men. Do you remember what Peter says? "We did not follow cleverly devised myths" (2 Peter 1:16). The Greek classics are fun to read. The Greek mythological texts are well constructed. They are cleverly devised. In the final analysis, however, they're myths and human constructs. They are of human origin. Contrary to the words of men, Peter says this Word, the Bible, came from above.

But what Paul and his fellow Apostles and authors of the New Testament had to offer was not some novel, cleverly crafted scheme. As Paul says, the message he preached, and the message the Thessalonian believers received, was the Word of God. It really was the Word of God. Against the words of men, there is the Word of God.

Paul puts it this way: "When you received the word of God, which you heard from us, you accepted it not as the word of men but as what it really is. . . ." So now he's going to define what that word is that he preached. It is, he tells us, "the word of God."

Peter Martyr Vermigli was born in Florence and came under the influence of the writings of the Reformers. He converted and fled. He spent time in the great Reformation cities of Switzerland before being invited to Cambridge. He also served at Oxford and then at Zurich. He was a staunch defender of the authority of Scripture. Vermigli said the authority of Scripture was established by two Latin words: *Dominus dixit*, translated as "thus says the Lord."[3] This is the starting point in our doctrine of Scripture. When we hear "thus says the Lord," we submit and we obey. The Bible is the Word of God.

Because it is the Word of God, it is powerful enough to do two things. It is powerful enough to have opened the eyes of those Thessalonian believers to the truth. And it is powerful enough to be "at work" in them.

Notice what Paul says next in 1 Thessalonians 2:13. He writes that this Word "is at work in you believers." That's the phrase we need to latch on to. The idea of the Word at work in us is akin to the goal of education. Education starts with *scientia*, or knowledge. But education must be more than a knowledge dump, like the transfer of data from one machine to another. Education also entails *sapientia*, or wisdom. We need to organize all the data and information. We need to be able to rank it or arrange it in a hierarchical fashion. We need wisdom to know how to apply information—and when to apply information. But education is more than wisdom. Education also entails, perhaps ultimately, *formatio*, or formation. Rivers are formed, carved out over time along the rock bed as water continually works on it. A carpenter forms a piece of wood into the desired shape for the desired function. The carpenter uses tools—the saw to cut away, the planer to shape and hone, the sandpaper to refine edges and smooth surfaces. Formation, in other words, can hurt.

Martin Luther once said that the Word of God assaults us. It takes off the rough edges, cuts away, and hones us to God's desired shape. We are cast in the image of the first man, Adam. We are being refashioned after the image of the last Man. We are being conformed to His image. Luther was right. The Word of God assaults us. Luther quickly added, however, that the Word of God comforts us. Whether assaulting or comforting, the Word of God is at work in shaping and forming us.

This is God's Word. We can put our confidence in it because it is God's Word to us. It is not a human construct. It is not some philosophy that's going to pass. It abides through the ages. To put the matter differently, the Bible is the only book powerful enough to change lives. And it is powerful enough because it really is the Word of God.

We can put our confidence in God's Word because it accomplishes what it sets out to do. To affirm this, we sometimes look to Isaiah 55:11:

> So shall my word be that goes out from my mouth;
> it shall not return to me empty,
> but it shall accomplish that which I purpose,
> and shall succeed in the thing for which I sent it.

This verse is reassuring enough. When we look at this verse in context, the impact becomes even more meaningful. In chapter two and in our look at our confidence in God, we examined the prophecy of God's promise to bring Israel back to the land after their exile. This is the same context for Isaiah 55. Freeing Israel from their captors and returning the entire nation is a rather big thing. Of course, the return from exile is but a shadow that hinted at an even larger undertaking, the fulfillment of all of God's promises to His people to restore Eden and to gently lead them into the new heavens and the new earth. God's gargantuan promises are not empty words. They will come to pass. So too will the small promises. So, too, will all of God's Word.

Consider the fuller context of Isaiah 55:11 by pondering verses 10–13:

For as the rain and the snow come down from heaven
    and do not return there but water the earth,
making it bring forth and sprout,
    giving seed to the sower and bread to the eater,
so shall my word be that goes out from my mouth;
    it shall not return to me empty,
but it shall accomplish that which I purpose,
    and shall succeed in the thing for which I sent it.

For you shall go out in joy
    and be led forth in peace;
the mountains and the hills before you
    shall break forth into singing,

and all the trees of the field shall clap their hands.
Instead of the thorn shall come up the cypress;
   instead of the brier shall come up the myrtle;
and it shall make a name for the Lord,
   an everlasting sign that shall not be cut off.

God's Word will come to pass. What He declares and what He promises will happen. His promises will be fulfilled in ways that will astound us and fill us with joy. His promises are certain and sure, firm and forever. When we rest in God's Word, all of our anxieties begin to melt away and we are at peace.

Does It Still Work?

Can God's Word calm the anxieties of our time? Does it bring us peace now, in the complexities of our age? Many voices clamor for our attention in our time. We are surrounded by screens and devices. We are talked to all the time. These voices try to pull us away from the clear and certain voice of God. We are living in an age where God's Word is continuously called into question. Where it is not only seen as unhelpful, but where it is also seen as a source of bigotry, intolerance, and narrow-minded, obsolete thinking. *Look forward, don't look back,* goes the mantra.

Can we trust the Bible? That is one question. But we are living in an age where the culture around us is asking, "Can we trust those who read the Bible? Aren't they dangerous?" That is to say, we will continually feel the pressure from our culture to privatize everything we believe, never speaking out for our beliefs and for our biblical convictions. We will also continually feel the pressure to compromise those beliefs and convictions, if not throw them overboard altogether.

We can have our Bible, but we can't take it seriously, our culture tells us. We certainly can't impose what the Bible teaches upon others. As long as we keep our beliefs to ourselves, everything will be all right.

These attacks from our culture come from confusing the Bible as merely some system of thought or some human ideology.

Suppose we become advocates of the medical practice of bloodletting. This was rather popular, even into the eighteenth century. If we practiced bloodletting in that era, no one would think anything of it. But if a doctor were to propose a return to this (very flawed) medical practice, he would be rightfully drummed out, if not prosecuted. Bloodletting was an ideology. Like all ideologies, it came and it went. Systems of thought, ideologies, views—they all come and go. Some are even useful and helpful. But, they have their day and then they pass.

When we open our Bibles, however, we are engaging something entirely different. We are not listening to the words of ancient men from some quaint faraway place and time. We are reading the very words of God. We can't simply ignore or pass over—or flat-out reject—the Bible because it is out of step with our day.

Jonathan Edwards once said, "The wisdom of God was not given for any particular age, but for all ages. It surely therefore becomes us to receive what God reveals to be truth and to look upon His Word."[4]

We sometimes have the wrong impression of Jonathan Edwards and the times in which he lived. He was born in 1703. He spent most of his life in Puritan New England. He moved to Princeton, New Jersey, in January 1758. For a very brief time, he served as president of Princeton University. He died on March 22, 1758, from complications related to a smallpox vaccination.

His portrait has him in a powdered wig with Geneva bands on his black robe, indicating his vocation as pastor. He looks like a Puritan. He looks like he lived in a Puritan bubble, preaching to Puritans, living among Puritans, reading Puritans . . . you get the picture.

In reality, however, his life was rather different. During most of his pastoral stay at his church in Northampton, Massachusetts, his congregation ran from its Puritan heritage. The people pursued their own agendas and their own self-interests, paying little heed to living out the truths their pastor put before them each week.

In 1734 and 1735, Jonathan Edwards and the congregation at Northampton experienced a revival. So did many other churches in the Connecticut River Valley in the colonies of Connecticut and Massachusetts. In the fall of 1733, Edwards preached some hard-hitting sermons. One of them, preached in November 1733, has been titled "The Kind of Preaching People Want." Edwards starts his sermon in the Old Testament, observing that God's people have had no shortage of false prophets, "that always flattered them in their sins." True prophets rebuke the sinner. False prophets leave sinners "to the peaceable enjoyment of their sins." He then turns to the desire that people in his own day had for such false prophets. Edwards continues,

"If ministers were sent to tell the people that they might gratify their lusts without danger . . . how eagerly would they be listened to by some, and what good attention they would give." He adds, "They would like a savior to save them in their sins much better than a savior to save them from their sins."[5]

Edwards was responding to those of his day who thought they knew better than the Word of God. He also wrote treatises to respond to the academics who thought they knew better than God's Word. The English academic world of Edwards' day was enthralled with the new thinking of the Enlightenment. The deists ruled. They believed that God created the world and then backed away, and now He lets it run along all on its own. They rejected the idea that God reveals His will in His Word. They rejected the doctrine of the incarnation and the deity of Christ. They rejected the possibility, let alone the actual occurrence, of miracles. They had "come of age." The Enlightenment thinkers and the deists were far too sophisticated to submit to some ancient book.

The philosophers had affected the church. In 1727, a group of independent ministers met in London to debate the deity of Christ. These were the exact descendants of the stalwart Puritans of the 1600s. They voted on the deity of Christ, and the deity of Christ lost. These were men who should have known better. They capitulated to the whims of the day.

Edwards kept up with these developments. He was not a backwoods minister. He had the latest books and kept current with the latest ideas. He saw where these ideas would take the church in the American Colonies. He sounded the alarm.

He also saw how his congregation could be so easily led astray by the wrong pursuits. He saw how worldliness crouched at the door, ready to overtake those who so willingly gave in.

So, he was not in a Puritan bubble. He responded to his culture and to his congregation. He preached sermons and he wrote books—all defending the Bible.

We are not historically situated at the dawn of the Enlightenment as Edwards was. We find our place at the Enlightenment's setting sun. We live in the dawn of postmodernism. We live among those who reject the Bible. We live among those who give in to the clutches of worldliness. Sin crouches at our door too.

So what pastoral counsel did Edwards offer? He pointed his congregation to the Bible. He argued against the Enlightenment thinkers and against the deist theologians based on the Bible. He looked to the Word.

As Edwards noted, the Bible belongs to every age. It is not simply the true Word for the first century. It is not simply the authoritative Word for the first century. It is not simply the necessary Word for the first century. It is not simply the sufficient Word for the first century.

It is the true, authoritative, necessary, clear, and sufficient Word for all centuries, including the twenty-first. Theologians sometimes speak of these as the attributes of Scripture. As the attributes of God help us to learn about God, the attributes of Scripture help us learn about Scripture. The first and foremost attribute of Scripture is its authority. Scripture is authoritative. We again hear Peter Martyr Vermigli remind us that it all comes down to "Thus says the Lord." If Scripture is the Word of God, it's authoritative.

As we further develop the doctrine of the authority of Scripture, we see that we are talking about inerrancy and infallibility. These doctrines stem from the doctrine of inspiration. It's a very simple formula. Scripture is the Word of God. That's the doctrine of inspiration. It refers to verbal, plenary inspiration. *Verbal* means the very words of Scripture are inspired. *Plenary* means all of Scripture is inspired, not just matters of faith, but also matters of history, matters of Genesis 1–3. All of Scripture in each and every part is inspired. It is the Word of God. If it is the Word of God—verbal, plenary inspiration—then, and therefore, it is true. This is the doctrine of the inerrancy and infallibility of Scripture.

This is where we begin with the doctrine of Scripture. We begin with the authority of Scripture. Because of Scripture's authority, we speak of Scripture as necessary. As creatures, we do not need to hear from our fellow creatures. But we need to hear from our Creator. Scripture also has the attribute of clarity. It is clear. In its fundamental message, it is understandable. You don't need a decoder ring or secret tablets to figure the Bible out. Anyone with a modicum of intelligence can read the Bible and understand its basic message.

But there's one last attribute of Scripture that theologians speak of. It is the attribute of sufficiency. This is where the rubber meets the road. It's one thing to affirm inerrancy. It's another thing to believe that the Bible is sufficient for all of life and godliness. And it's another thing still to practice that.

It is one thing to affirm the inerrancy or authority of Scripture; the church also needs to speak to the challenges to Scripture's authority in the public square. And we need to do the same in our families, in our neighborhoods, and in the circles where we live and work. We need to defend the authority of Scripture. Too many self-professed evangelicals are weakening their stance on inerrancy and on authority. We must hold that line, no matter what challenges come our way.

But there is another concern and another task for the church. As the standing of Scripture in culture is eroded, we can be subtly moved to look away from it. We begin to wonder if Scripture truly does have all the answers. We begin to wonder if all of Scripture's answers are right. Maybe Scripture is not so sufficient anymore. Life in the twenty-first century is so complex. The problems we are dealing with are so complex that we need to look elsewhere, we might think. All of a sudden, we are affirming the authority of Scripture in our doctrinal statements while denying the authority of Scripture in our daily lives.

The temptation is to think the Bible has run its course. The temptation is to think it is helpful and inspiring, and to think that *at certain times, in certain places, and on certain topics* it is true. But not entirely true. We must consider one simple observation, however: Scripture cannot be partially inspired; neither can it be partially authoritative. The moment we speak of "partly," we are the ones who decide which parts. We are setting ourselves over Scripture as the authority. The doctrine of the authority and inerrancy of Scripture is not like hand grenades or a game of horseshoes. Close does not count.

Since the Bible is the Word of God, we must take it seriously. We must take all of it seriously. We must listen to it, submit to it, and follow it. Many of our brothers and sisters in Christ from previous centuries faced persecution for their biblical convictions. Many of our brothers and sisters around the globe today face persecution for their biblical convictions. The time may very likely come for us in the American church to face persecution, as well.

The temptation to accommodate to culture rather than follow God's Word will likely increase and intensify in the days and years ahead. The temptation for most of us will not be to outright deny the Bible. Some will do that, and the consequences will be tragic. But it's a rather obvious temptation and most of us would not entertain it. The temptation will be more subtle. The temptation will be simply to disregard its teachings. We may never deny the Bible, but we may very well simply disregard its teachings. These temptations to drift from God's Word have dogged us ever since the garden of Eden. Yet there is an urgency in our day. We must not lull ourselves into a complacency or seek a false assurance. In numerous places, the New Testament authors warn us to not grow slack in our fight against temptation, and they warn us to not be naive. May we heed their warning. Instead of drifting from the Bible, may we run to it and cling to it. May we be confident in the Bible and trust in it, no matter the consequence.

The Beauty of Scripture

In addition to the four traditional attributes of Scripture, there is at least one more: beauty. Scripture is beautiful, pure, radiant,

and lovely. We see this attribute of Scripture reflected throughout Scripture's pages. The beauty of Scripture, however, shines
no more splendidly than in the Psalms. The psalmists love God's
Word; they admire it. They desire it and long for it as their very
sustenance. The longest psalm, Psalm 119, is one long hymn to
the Bible's power, authority, and beauty. As such, it is not a word
for the past but truly a word for every age.

Psalm 119 teaches us at least one thing that is counterintuitive: affliction and persecution are good things. Before we
proceed to explore this, however, some opening comments are
in order. The psalmist doesn't go seeking after persecution and
affliction. We see this even in the early church under Rome's
watch. When the arrest warrant was issued for Polycarp, he
went on the run, hiding in place after place until he was caught.
None of these early Christians walked into the arena and asked
to be thrown to the beasts. Facing affliction and persecution
does not mean seeking it out or bringing it on.

Second, not all Christians are called to affliction and persecution. Did not Paul himself say that the lesson of contentment
is learned both in times of need and in times of plenty?

In the 1620s and 1630s, many Puritan ministers were ejected
from England and sent into exile either in the Netherlands or
in the New World. But in the 1640s, as Parliament gained the
upper hand, they were brought back, some rather ceremoni-
ously. Jeremiah Burroughs had lost his pulpit and was exiled
to Rotterdam in 1637. Then, in 1641, he was invited back and
found himself delivering a sermon before Parliament.

One of Burroughs' most helpful books is his little treasure

called *The Rare Jewel of Christian Contentment.*[6] We are called to be faithful in season and out of season. Not all Christians are called to affliction and persecution. Sometimes, living as faithful disciples is difficult in the good times.

We need to keep some of these principles in mind as we explore the biblical teaching on affliction and persecution and as we consider our own context today and what may very well lie on the horizon for us. The overwhelming majority of Christians have experienced being out of step with culture and the powers to be, rather than being in step and accepted.

This was true of the author of Psalm 119. In this long hymn to the Word of God, the psalmist declares:

Even though princes sit plotting against me,
    your servant will meditate on your statutes.
Your testimonies are my delight;
    they are my counselors. (vv. 23–24)

And declares:

Let your steadfast love come to me, O LORD,
    your salvation according to your promise;
then shall I have an answer for him who taunts me,
    for I trust in your word. (vv. 41–42)

And declares:

I will also speak of your testimonies before kings
    and shall not be put to shame,

for I find my delight in your commandments,
    which I love. (vv. 46–47)

And declares again:

This is my comfort in my affliction,
    that your promise gives me life.
    The insolent utterly deride me,
    but I do not turn away from your law.
When I think of your rules from of old,
    I take comfort, O LORD.
Hot indignation seizes me because of the wicked,
    who forsake your law. (vv. 50–52)

Like a multifaceted diamond, the twenty-two stanzas of Psalm 119 reveal the depths and contours of the beauty and truthfulness of God's special revelation—a beauty that sustains and comforts in the face of persecution, affliction, and derision. In each stanza, the psalmist puts our eyes squarely on God's Word that is forever and firmly fixed in the heavens (v. 89).

The Bible *really is* God's Word. May we receive it for what it really is and put our confidence in it.

Chapter Four

CONFIDENCE
IN CHRIST

How extensive is the kingdom of King Herod now?
How extensive is the kingdom of King Jesus now?

—SINCLAIR B. FERGUSON

Forbid it, Lord, that I should boast
save in the death of Christ my God.

—ISAAC WATTS

When Martin Luther decided to address the crisis in the church of his day, he took the approach of a scholar. He sat at his desk and penned a series of points, or theses, for public debate. The church of his day taught everyone from princes to paupers that they needed to look for comfort to the saints, relics, priests, and even flimsy pieces of paper that promised redemption and peace with God. This teaching left Luther entirely without peace, disillusioned, and even on the verge of depression.

None of those things, Luther argued, deserve our attention or even a passing glance. In fact, all of those things obscure the one thing we should be looking at: Christ, and at that, Christ on the cross.

Thesis 37

Luther posted his Ninety-Five Theses on the Castle Church door in Wittenberg on October 31, 1517.[1] Of these, two in particular help focus our attention on Christ and the cross. Thesis 37 reads, "Every true Christian, whether living or dead, has part in all the benefits of Christ and the church; and this is granted to him by God, even without letters of pardon."

In this thesis, Luther uses a beautiful Latin phrase that has quite a history: *participatio omnium bonorum Christi.* Luther first came across this phrase in the writings of Thomas Aquinas. The Reformers would take this phrase and run with it—all the way to the profound doctrine of union with Christ. Being in Christ means we participate in all of the benefits that are His. Even as Christ was being lowered from the cross, the Father cared for Him. And at the resurrection, the Father exalted Him and lavished all of His love and all that He has to offer upon Him. We are joint heirs with Him. What does it mean to be "in Christ"? It means we are blessed beyond measure, blessed beyond comprehension.

Luther also turns our attention to the cross in the final theses of his history-changing work. In theses 92 and 93, he intones, "Away then, with all those prophets who say to the people of Christ, 'Peace,

peace' and there is no peace! Blessed be all those prophets who say to the people of Christ, 'Cross, cross, and there is no cross!'"

Luther here echoes the prophet Jeremiah. A false prophet falsely assures people of a false peace. "You're OK," says the prophet. In reality, you are not OK. In fact, you are so far from OK you can't even see it. And so you are not at peace.

The true prophet says "cross." The true prophet points people to Christ and to what Christ did on the cross. So what does Luther mean when he says, "There is no cross"? He means there is no cross for us. There is nothing left for us to do. Christ has done it all. He bore the cross and He accomplished it all. Christ's own words spoken from the cross put the exclamation point on it all: "It is finished."

At a time of both intense personal conflict and intense conflict within the church, Luther looked to Christ and looked to Christ on the cross. We speak of the Reformation battle cry of *sola fide* (faith alone) and *sola gratia* (grace alone). In truth, these are shorthand for *solus Christus* (Christ alone). There were so many distractions, so many false places where people had placed their confidence. The Reformers simplified things. The Reformers brought a laser focus to the singular issue that makes the difference. Our confidence must be in Christ.

The author of Hebrews does the exact same thing. Hebrews is unlike any other epistle in the New Testament. It's anonymous, and it lacks the typical greeting found in all the other Epistles. But its rhetoric soars. The opening verses are a literary work of art and contain theology so well presented that it stirs the mind and soul. The author immediately casts our eyes upon Christ, "the radiance of the glory of God" (1:3). In chapter 2, the author reveals his concern for the audience. He implores them to pay attention lest they drift away (v. 1). And with these two chapters as his introduction, he turns to his main theme in chapter 3, verses 1–6. The theme of this tour de force may be summed up in two words—two words that call us to a singular action: Consider Jesus.

We find the same words at the end of the book in chapter 12, verse 3. We must consider Jesus. As we read Hebrews, we find why we need to consider Jesus. The author is deeply concerned that the audience of his book not drift away. The church faced enemies without and enemies within. Rome was a formidable enemy without. As a superpower, it wielded great force, and it unleashed that force on the new sect called Christians. The church of the New Testament and the church of the early centuries was a persecuted church.

The enemy within posed an equally formidable threat. Apostasy and false teachers threatened to lead people astray. So the author of Hebrews implores his audience to stand firm, to hold fast, to never waver, and to never cower. In fact, the author tells us to "hold fast our confidence" (3:6). That confidence is in Christ. One chapter later, again, the author of Hebrews tells us to "hold fast our confession" and to draw near to the throne of grace "with confidence" (4:14–16).

The Perfecter of the Faith

What do we find when we consider Christ? We find that He is truly God (1:1–3). We find that He is truly man (2:17–18).

We find that He is our High Priest who is able to save to the uttermost (4:14–16; 7:25; 10:11–14). We find that He is superior to everything else that precedes Him. We find that He is the God-man who accomplished our salvation through His perfect obedience and atoning death on the cross. Christ is the complete revelation of God, He is the complete fulfillment and apex of all revelation, and He is the consummation of all God's promises. If all we had was the book of Hebrews, how much would we know about Christ? Enough to cause us to wonder in amazement and to worship Him in adoration forever.

The author circles through these themes throughout the book and then again commends us to look to Jesus, "the founder and perfecter of our faith" (12:2). Notice, then, the three things we are told:

1. Jesus endured the cross.
2. Jesus despised the shame.
3. Jesus is vindicated as He is seated at the right hand of the Father.

The cross was the Roman symbol of shame, reserved for the most heinous of criminals and the very dregs of society. Jesus was cast out, rejected. He was shamed to an extent that is barely imaginable, let alone experienced by the vast majority of human beings. In spite of this, however, He won the victory, He was vindicated, and He is exalted.

As we consider Christ who endured (12:3), we then can endure (v. 7). Again, the author of Hebrews soars rhetorically: "Therefore lift your drooping hands and strengthen your weak knees, and make straight paths for your feet, so that what is lame may not be put out of joint but rather be healed" (vv. 12–13).

To an audience that faced enemies without and within, to an audience on shaky ground, to a feeble and frail audience, the author of Hebrews simply says, "Consider Jesus." When we do, we can stand fast. When we do, we can have confidence.

We see the same thing in 1 Peter. Chapter 3 speaks of our enemies and of those who challenge the faith. Peter here speaks of the suffering of his audience for righteousness' sake. In light of this opposition, he tells them: "Have no fear of them, nor be troubled, but in your hearts honor Christ the Lord as holy, always being prepared to make a defense to anyone who asks you for a reason for the hope that is within you; yet do it with gentleness and respect" (vv. 14b–15).

We usually turn to this verse to talk about apologetics, the defense of the faith. But here we see Peter telling us where to stand when suffering comes and when opposition comes. Honoring Christ the Lord as holy in our hearts stresses the importance and necessity of our identity in Christ. This is who we are. We are in Christ. Therefore, we can stand firm.

SPQR

Peter unpacks for us what it means to be in Christ, what it means to participate in all His benefits. In 1 Peter 2:9, he tells us we "are a chosen race, a royal priesthood, a holy nation, people for [God's] own possession." We were not a people (2:10). We were hopeless and floundering. Now, we are a people.

If you lived in first-century Rome, you would have seen four initials almost everywhere. Even modern-day travelers to the city of Rome see this phrase. It is beneath their feet, on the manhole covers, as they walk on ancient streets. The four initials are *SPQR*. The initials represent a Latin phrase, *Senatus Populusque Romanus*, meaning "the Senate and people of Rome." These ubiquitous initials stressed the benefits of one's identity as a citizen of Rome. Great privilege came with being Roman, great pride stemming from a long and legendary history. SPQR—*we are Roman and all of this is ours.*

Peter gives us a far greater identity, of far greater privilege, and of far greater legend. Consider the adjectives: *chosen, royal,* and *holy.* Consider the nouns: *race, priesthood, nation, people.* We are all of this as the people of God—in and through Christ.

Being a Roman citizen involved more than simply the bestowal of privilege. It also entailed obligation. To be a Roman meant to live like a Roman. So it is in 1 Peter with our citizenship in Christ. It places us in a position of privilege *and it also obligates us.* In short, the obligation is to be holy (1:15). Throughout the epistle, Peter fleshes out this broad command to be holy in many particular obligations. See 1 Peter 2:11–17 for a list, among other places in the epistle.

Peter also uses our identity in Christ to teach us one more thing. We will suffer persecution. We should "not be surprised at the fiery trial when it comes" (4:12). We should not be shaken. Instead, we must stand firm (5:12). As with the book of Hebrews, we again see this recurring concept: *Consider Jesus— and when you do, stand firm.*

Read the New Testament while looking for this one-two punch and you will find it spilling all over the pages. We must consider Jesus because our challenges are so great. We can stand firm because Jesus is so much greater. We could put this another way. What do we learn from the authors of the New Testament Epistles about what is important for the church and for the Christian life? Invariably, we learn that they desire for us to stand firm and hold fast. Why is this their concern? Because the opposition is great, because there are challenges, and because the Christian life is difficult. We have challenges from without, from culture. We have challenges from within the church, from false teachers. We also have challenges from within ourselves, from our sin nature.

But the biblical authors not only tell us to stand firm, they tell us, as we have been seeing, where we need to stand. We don't stand upon our status in society. We don't stand upon our own strength or abilities. We stand firm in Christ and we stand firm in the gospel.

Our challenges are great, but Christ and the gospel are so much greater. The urgency is also great.

The two days of April 17–18, 1521, at the Diet of Worms were a defining moment in the life of Martin Luther. He thought he would finally get his debate with the church. He did not get a debate. Instead, the officials called upon him to recant, to renounce his writings. Luther asked for one day to respond. He spent the night agonizing in prayer. The sun came up and the next day came and Luther, in his simple monk's robe, appeared before the imperial diet with all the church and court officials arrayed in the trappings of their office, all lined up against the solitary monk. Again, the officials asked Luther, "Do you recant?" Luther then delivered his famous speech:

> Your Imperial Majesty and Your Lordships demand a simple answer. Here it is, plain and unvarnished. Unless I am convinced of error by the testimony of Scripture or, since I put no trust in the unsupported authority of Pope or councils, since it is plain that they have often erred and often contradicted themselves, by manifest reasoning, I stand convinced by the Scriptures to which I have appealed. My conscience is captive to the Word of God. To go against conscience is neither safe for us, nor open to us. I cannot and will not recant anything.
>
> Here I stand. I can do no other. God help me. Amen.[2]

I have heard R.C. Sproul speak of this moment in Luther's life many times. He has Luther's speech memorized and knows the events of that moment down to every textured detail. R.C. explains what Luther's famous line means: "When Luther said, 'Here I stand,' he wasn't standing still. He was standing firm." We stand firm, and as Sproul continues to say, we stand firm not just for today, and not just for tomorrow, but for the sake of generations, even centuries, to come. Standing firm means advancing and looking ahead. Our current time is not a time for retreat. We cannot even afford the status quo. Our time urgently calls for advance.

But what does that advance look like? To help answer this question, consider a quote by Dietrich Bonhoeffer. He once said, "A king who dies on a cross must be the king of a rather strange kingdom."[3] Bonhoeffer points us in the right direction.

The Fellowship of His Sufferings

We have been looking at this richly contoured doctrine of union with Christ. Because we are united with Christ, we, then, are brought in to participate in the full benefits of that which Christ receives and which Christ has. We like to celebrate that.

Paul helps us see this in Philippians 3:10. In the first half of this verse, we see what it means to be in Christ and what it means to participate in all that He accomplished. Paul yearns that he "may know Him and the power of His resurrection." If only there were a period right there, what a wonderful verse this would be. But there is no period. Paul proceeds to tell us something that we need to think about, despite the fact that we don't like to think about it. Paul goes on to say that we "may share his sufferings, becoming like him in his death."

We cling to the part of union with Christ that means forgiveness of sins, that means the conquering of all of our enemies, including sin and death, and that means ultimate victory. We like that we are raised in newness of life in Christ. Yet being united with Christ also means that we share in His sufferings and that, as Paul says here, we become "like him in his death." What does this mean?

The Cool Table

When we consider our current time, what are the implications of Paul's teachings here for us? If we think specifically in terms of North American Christianity and evangelicalism, we can think in terms of the last generation. Using a forty-year span, we can consider American evangelicals from the 1970s through the 2000s.

Looking back over that generation, we see the rise of the Jesus People. The Jesus People were known by their sign, the index finger pointing up, signifying "the One Way." Many of these Jesus People were formerly hippies. Many were musicians. So in this same moment, we see the beginnings of the Contemporary Christian Music movement, which would come to make up a major share of the market in the American music world and would launch an entire Christian product industry.

We also see this generation coming out from under the cloud that had hung over conservative Christians ever since the days of the Scopes Trial. After that moment in 1925, theologically conservative Christians were marginalized in culture and even sounded a retreat of sorts. All of a sudden, however, in 1976, *Time* magazine—not a conservative magazine at all— declared that year "the Year of the Evangelical." We had arrived. The man sitting behind the desk in the Oval Office claimed to be born again, and everyone loved Billy Graham. The 1980s only seemed to get better.

Looking back over the generation of the 1970s through the 2000s, one could say that evangelicals had influence, politically and culturally. Some who look back now wonder how deep that influence actually ran. Some have even spoken of that moment

as "the myth of influence." Nevertheless, evangelicals and conservative Christians enjoyed a certain place in American culture
during that era.

Now, we are in the 2010s and looking ahead to the next generation. If this first decade of the next generation is any indicator
of where things are going, we will find ourselves in a very different cultural location than the immediately prior generation.

I am reminded of my days in junior high and of the "cool
table" in the cafeteria. Everyone wanted a seat at the cool table—
or, at least, everyone acted as if they did. Evangelicals might
have been at the cool table at various moments from the 1970s
to the 2000s, but we're finding now that the cool table no longer
wants us there.

Russell Moore explains this shifting dynamic with an anec-
dote concerning a college friend. A few years ago, this friend
called Moore to ask him for a church recommendation. Dr.
Moore replied with joy in his voice, expressing how wonderful
it was to hear that his old friend had become a Christian. The
former classmate quickly assured him, however, that he was not
a Christian. Rather, he was running for political office, and he
knew that he had to be a member of a good church in order to
have a fighting chance at the polls. That was then. Moore now
observes that church membership may very well be a detriment
at the polls. Moore further points out that this is not such a bad
thing. Opportunists will not inherit the kingdom of heaven, to
paraphrase the Gospels. This new cultural shakeout in our day
may have a healthy winnowing effect. This may be the proverbial silver lining in the cloud.

But there is still the cloud. We are finding ourselves in this new, different, and disorienting cultural moment. We're finding that the cool table no longer wants us sitting there. And so we have new questions to ask about what it means to be a Christian in culture. This cultural shakeout might very well be a good thing. The tremors of it may shake out those structures that are "culturally Christian" or nominally Christian, leaving behind an edifice that is biblically Christian.

We also may find ourselves in very good company. In many ways, we may have more in common with the church of the New Testament era than with previous generations of the American church or the church in the West. Many of our brothers and sisters in Christ around the globe experience firsthand the persecution and cultural marginalization that we read of time and time again in the pages of the New Testament. Their experiences resonate directly with the experiences of the believers of the New Testament era.

As we see the shifts and fissures in our day, we may find that our lives and experiences resonate more and more with the lives and experiences of the church of the New Testament. Ultimately, we may find ourselves in the company of our Savior, the King who died on a cross, and the King of that rather strange kingdom Bonhoeffer mentioned.

For us, this cultural marginalization might be a bit of a new thing. Suffering and persecution are new waters that we are entering in this new cultural context for the American church or the church in the West. As we move into what is being called more and more a "post-Christian" culture, are we going to find that this expression that we "share in his sufferings" might resonate a little more deeply with our experience? We might gain some firsthand experience of what it means to "become like him in his death."

We have made the cross into a fine piece of jewelry. Shaped of precious metals, jeweled, it hangs on chains around people's necks. It was an execution symbol in the first century. Derek Thomas once compared it to hanging a syringe or an electric chair pendant on a chain. Not only did the cross represent execution, it was reserved for executing the lowest of the low. In Roman culture, the cross was very simply a symbol of shame. The cross represented the ultimate social outcast who was pushed not only to the margins, but even outside of the margins. This symbol stands at the center of our identity as a church. Jesus uses it to express the essence of discipleship (Matt. 16:24).

The cross is a symbol of shame and a symbol of weakness. When we say our confidence must be in Christ, we are saying something rather multidimensional. On the one hand, we see that Christ currently reigns as King. We speak of Christ as holding the threefold office—prophet, priest, and king—and so, as King, He reigns. He reigns over all things. And that is certainly a basis for us to have confidence. Christ is King. Christ rules. It's not that He will rule; He rules now. And so that's a basis for confidence.

But there's also another basis for confidence, and it concerns what the cross represents. Embracing shame, suffering, persecution, and opposition seems entirely counterintuitive. We tend to seek pleasure and avoid pain. So, participating in the fellowship of Christ's sufferings strikes us as counterintuitive and counterproductive. It is also countercultural. Here we learn something profound about weakness.

Not only does Paul give us much to ponder in Philippians 3:10, he also offers his own experience in an intriguing autobiographical reflection in 2 Corinthians 12. This text likewise provides the opportunity for Paul to use his gift of sarcasm. We pick up hints of this sarcasm in places such as 2 Corinthians 11:5, where Paul speaks of "super-apostles." He considers the two chapters of 2 Corinthians 11–12 as an exercise in foolishness. He brags and boasts. All of this served to answer criticisms that were launched against Paul by his enemies and even by those who should have been his friends. But in this sarcasm and foolishness lies one of the most edifying texts in the writings of Paul.

By the time we get to 2 Corinthians, Paul has already informed us of many of his accomplishments. These accomplishments alone establish his credentials and should be sufficient to silence his adversaries. But Paul pivots in chapter 12 to something that astounds.

He recalls a vision that he had—a vision so intense and so visceral that it transcends expression and defies description. He saw and heard things beyond comprehension (vv. 2–4). Then, he plants his feet firmly on the earth to tell us of a "thorn in the flesh," his besetting weakness. We must note two things.

First, if it were you or me and our reputation and our claim to authority was on the line and being challenged, what would we choose to vindicate ourselves? Would we use the vision? Or, would we use the thorn and the weakness? We would use the vision. We would write our book on the experience of the few minutes in Paradise and we would line up seminars and we would make something of it. Not Paul. Paul actually brings up the vision so that he can move past it.

Paul uses the platform of his weakness to vindicate his authority and his ministry. That has to be the first thing we notice. The second thing we must notice is the cultural context and how that only serves to intensify Paul's use of the thorn over the transcendent experience.

Rome valued power and strength. Rome disdained weakness. We have mentioned this idea already, and this idea is crucial to understanding the cultural context of the New Testament books. That Christ died on a cross, that Christ is the leader of this new sect, and that His followers, called "Christians," have adopted the cross as their defining symbol—this all flies in the face of Rome's celebration of power and strength. Loving your enemies as a recurring Christian ethic? That, too, puts you out of step with Rome.

Now, here in 2 Corinthians 12, Paul plays the weakness card when he should have pulled out the strength card.

Rome valued the physical form, the powerful, the beautiful. Paul, from what we understand, lacked those qualities. He had the years and the mileage behind him. As we learn from 2 Corinthians 11, Paul had been shipwrecked, jailed, and beaten. He was lowered over a wall in a basket when his life was in danger. All of this had taken its toll. We get the impression that Paul failed to measure up to Roman standards for leaders in the category of appearance and platform presence.

Ultimately, we don't know what the "thorn in the flesh" was.

Paul does not tell us. We can only speculate. Barrels of ink have gone toward laying out various theories by numerous commentators. The truth is Paul does not tell us what it is. What he does say, however, needs to capture our attention.

Paul refused to welcome his thorn in the flesh. Three times, he pleaded that God would remove it. Paul wanted none of it. Then, Paul learned what God was teaching him through it. Charles Spurgeon once remarked, "We learn, I hope, something in the bright fields of joy, but I am more persuaded that we don't learn a tenth as much, there, as we do in the valley of Death-Shade." Paul's thorn sent him to school. Paul had been to school many times and had a great deal to show for it. But this school and this learning stand out.

When Paul realized that God would not remove the thorn, he learned something. In 2 Corinthians 12:9, Paul records the words that God directly spoke to him. As Paul writes these words, it's as if he's hearing them again and for the first time. Paul hears, "My grace is sufficient for you, for my power is made perfect in weakness."

All of these words come packed with significance:

My . . . This is from God, our God, who has brought us to Himself. The war is over and we are at peace with the holy God. God is not the distant, wholly other. Instead, He addresses Paul directly and with the personal pronoun.

Grace . . . Mercy would be cause for celebration enough, but God gives us riches beyond what we deserve. God is gracious, kind, good, and generous. Mercy holds back judgment. Grace goes above and beyond.

Sufficient . . . God knows us intimately. He knows how to meet our true needs.

Power . . . This word the Romans lusted after? God is the source. God's power makes Rome's look like a sandcastle.

Perfect . . . Pure and undefiled, without any flaw or blemish—what God does has full integrity and is done to the ultimate degree.

Weakness . . . We stand before God as feeble, frail, and unable. Yet, in and through God and by His grace, we overcome and rise above our weakness.

All of the words in this sentence have significance. But, I think the key word here is the verb. The key word is *is*.

We have mentioned two things we must notice in understanding this text. We see that Paul uses the thorn and not the vision to vindicate and assert his authority and ministry. We also see how this idea gets intensified when we consider the cultural context. There is a third thing we must also notice. The third thing is the chronology of this passage, and the meaning of *is*.

Paul mentions that this vision and this revelation came fourteen years ago (12:2). Paul wrote his second letter to the church at Corinth around AD 55. Going back fourteen years would take us to AD 41. Scholars have dated Paul's conversion to sometime between AD 33 and 36, with 34 as the most likely date.

The chronology means that Paul learned this intense and particular lesson regarding God's power and grace after he was converted. Seven years after Paul's conversion, God brought him back into the classroom for a most important lesson. God's grace and God's power are not there only at our conversion.

At our conversion, we recognize that we have come to the end of ourselves and realize our utter inability, and so we look to Christ. What Paul learns here is that we keep looking. We live the Christian life by grace and by God's power. Not only did Paul learn this important lesson seven years after his conversion, he also learned that God's grace *is* sufficient. The key word in this beautiful Mount Everest of texts is the present-tense verb. God's grace is not exclusive to the past. God's grace flows freely in the present and on into the future.

Two implications arise from this. One is that God's grace is sufficient to save, but it is also sufficient to keep us and to meet us at every turn as we live the Christian life.

This is one of the key lessons that John Bunyan's main character, Christian, learns as he makes his journey to the Celestial City in *The Pilgrim's Progress*. In the face of adversity piled upon adversity, Christian learns to depend on God's grace, to remember what happened when he came to the cross and his burden was rolled off his back, and to remember to look to Christ—not to his own strength. Again, thanks to Luther, we sing: "Did we in our strength confide? Our striving would be losing."

So the first implication is that we enter the Christian life entirely by God's grace and power, and so we live the Christian life by God's grace and power. The second implication is this: we are weak. We enter and live the Christian life by God's grace and power because there's no other way. We have nothing to offer and nothing to stand on in and of ourselves.

Admitting our weakness is key to putting our confidence in Christ. Admitting our weakness is key to learning what it means to fellowship with Christ's suffering and what it means to become like Him in His death.

Paul ends this autobiographical episode with this: "Therefore I will boast all the more gladly of my weaknesses, so that the power of Christ may rest upon me. For the sake of Christ, then, I am content with weaknesses, insults, hardships, persecutions, and calamities. For when I am weak, then I am strong" (12:9b–10).

This list strikes me as the exact opposite of the typical "Christmas letter." Do you know what I mean? Have you received letters during the holidays from friends or family members that list the great accomplishments of all their children that year? Letters that state that one child is off to study for the summer at Harvard, and then going with NASA to the International Space Station, and then will be celebrating his sixteenth birthday? Yes, those letters.

Imagine Paul's Christmas letter. Or, imagine Paul's missionary letter back to his supporting churches.

Dear Supporters,

This past year, I was persecuted and beaten a few times. There were many occasions where they kicked me out of the city. Also, sorry for how this looked in the press, but I was arrested and spent some time in jail. Did I mention the insults?

Yours truly,
Paul

In this litany of items mentioned by Paul, there is nothing that we like, nothing that, naturally speaking, we are drawn to or want to embrace. Yet, Paul tells us this not only characterizes his life and ministry, but this also enables his life and ministry to magnify Christ and magnify Christ's power.

Christ, too, suffered. They hurled insults at Him. Christ's weakness became readily apparent to all when He collapsed beneath the weight of the cross on His way to His death.

Christ's weakness began at the very beginning. He entered into this world, became incarnate, in weakness. Let's not forget that Mary was poor, and that the birth of Jesus came under suspicious—actually, scandalous—circumstances. Then there is the birth itself. Jesus, the Lord, did not enter this world in the rooms of a palace, but in the stall of an animal stable. And shortly after His birth, the megalomaniac Herod ordered the slaughter of the children of Jerusalem, and Rachel wept for her children (Matt. 2:13–23).

The Philadelphia Museum of Art houses Massimo Stanzione's version of *The Massacre of the Innocents*. Six-and-a-half feet tall, the Baroque painting stretches to just over ten feet wide. It is impressive, horrifically impressive. The mothers and infants are helpless at the precipice of utter despair. Anguish has twisted their faces. But the soldiers are finely tuned specimens of human strength, with chiseled muscles coiled to unleash brute force. You cannot walk by this painting; you must stop. A mere painting of this horror leaves you stunned. Yet, the slaughter of the innocents was a real event.

Joseph and Mary took their infant son and fled to the deserts of Egypt. Decades later, in a desert in the wilderness, Jesus faced the severest of temptations. When the time came for Jesus to announce His public ministry, calamities and persecution followed. In Jesus' darkest hour, His closest friends and confidants abandoned Him. Looking in at the incarnate Christ affords many opportunities to see hardships and calamities, insults and persecutions, and demonstrations of weakness.

When we consider the incarnate Christ, what do we see? We do not see an aloof High Priest. We see one who was made perfect through suffering (Heb. 2:10). We see a High Priest entirely sympathetic with our weakness. We see that He has passed through not the mere shadow of the valley of death, but through death itself. We are led to see that His strength and His power shine in our weakness.

So We Endure

At the end of his magisterial work the *Institutes of the Christian Religion*, Calvin turns his attention to the civil government. The very last chapter of the last book of the *Institutes*—book four, chapter twenty—concerns our lives as citizens in the civic sphere. Calvin acknowledges that this may appear out of place, but only at first glance. He informs us, "For although this topic seems by nature alien to the spiritual doctrine of faith which I have undertaken to discuss, what follows will show that I am right in joining them, in fact, that necessity compels me to do so." Calvin thinks it necessary because the civil government is ordained by God and of very useful purposes. Calvin reports that civil government "provides that a public manifestation of religion may exist among Christians, and that humanity be maintained among men."[4]

Calvin wants to help his readers apply all of the theology he has been teaching them from book one, chapter one, all the way through to book four, chapter nineteen. He wants his readers to see how they can live theologically and apply theology to the issues surrounding them as they live in the world.

As he unpacks the Christian's relationship to the state, he informs us that the civil magistrate is ordained by God, that it has the right to exercise force and administer punishment, and that government can even levy taxes. He engages the issue of the relationship of civil laws to biblical laws and of the Christian's obligation to obedience. Calvin helps us understand how to live well and wisely as citizens.

Then, he tells us this: "For truly, Christians ought to be a kind of men born to bear slander, and injuries; open to malice and deceits, mockeries of wicked men. And not that only, but they ought to bear patiently all these evils. That is, they should have such complete spiritual composure that, having received one offense, they make ready for another, promising themselves throughout life nothing but the bearing of a perpetual cross."[5]

Calvin is onto something here regarding our union with Christ and regarding placing our confidence in Christ regardless of what the external outcome is and regardless of what the cultural priorities are.

Calvin also addresses the potential conflict between obedience to human government and obedience to God's law. Following biblical teaching and example, such as that of Peter in Acts 5:29, he declares that we must follow God. Then, Calvin foresees a time when such conflict will come. Calvin assumes that Christians will "suffer anything rather than turn aside from piety."[6] He counsels that in such times, we will find comfort in our obedience to God.

This must not be glossed over. This is from the very last paragraph of the *Institutes*. When the time of conflict comes, the conflict that pits God's directives in Scripture against the laws of the land, the Christian must not compromise, must never cower. Instead, the Christian must stand with God's law—no matter the consequences. May we be much more willing to "suffer anything" than "turn away from piety." Calvin then adds a final plea "that our courage may not grow faint." He then offers his final charge: "We have been redeemed by Christ at so great a price as our redemption cost him, so that we should not enslave ourselves to the wicked desires of men—much less be subject to their impiety."[7]

There are indeed many dimensions to the doctrine of our union with Christ. Being in Christ is our identity. It gives us privileges and standing. It also brings obligations—obligations to bear our cross as Christ bore His. What does it mean to share in Christ's sufferings? It means a counterintuitive and countercultural way of life.

In Christ: The Admirable Conjunction of Divine Excellencies

Martin Luther preached his last sermon on January 17, 1546, at the *Schlosskirche*, the Castle Church, in Wittenberg. Right afterward, he learned of a crisis back in Eisleben, the town of his birth. Luther was an old man. Like Paul, Luther had both the years and the mileage racked up. On that day in January, Luther wrote a letter in which he declared himself to be "old, weary, lazy, worn out, cold, chilly and, over and above, a one-eyed man."[8] Luther likely had cataracts—a true thorn in the flesh for a scholar and one who lived among books and writing. One eye was glossed over. He finished the letter with the wish that "half dead, as I am, I might be left in peace."

Luther would not be left in peace. He was summoned to Eisleben to solve the crisis there. Though relatively short, the journey to get there had its share of terrors and difficulties. Ice floes in the Elbe River, which he had to cross, had knocked off part of the dock, keeping the boat from landing its passengers safely and dry. Luther and his party landed on the bank. They and everything with them got wet and then froze in the chilled air. Luther's age made him susceptible to these conditions and circumstances. He fell ill, likely of pneumonia. He and his party eventually made it to Eisleben. Luther recovered measures of health here and there, but could not shake the illness that slowly seized ground.

Meanwhile, word of Luther's ill health made its way back to his beloved wife, Katie, in Wittenberg. She anxiously wrote to her husband, expressing her wish that she could take care of him. Luther replied that he had a better caretaker than her, even one better than the angels. Luther, the dying old man, wrote that he had a caretaker who "lies in a manger and nurses at His mother's breast. Yet, He sits at the right hand of God the Father Almighty."

There is an irony here. A helpless babe is our strength, our comforter, and our deliverer. Remember when Ruth, the foreigner who married Boaz, gave birth to Obed? When that event occurred, the women of Bethlehem came to the old widow Naomi and told her that a son was born to her, one who would deliver her and nourish her in her old age (Ruth 4:13–17). Remember when the angels appeared to the shepherds on a hillside outside of that very same city? When that event occurred, the angels told the shepherds to go find a babe lying in a manger. They told them that the baby is the Savior (Luke 2:8–19).

Jonathan Edwards once wrote of the "admirable conjunction of divine excellencies in Christ Jesus." Christ was truly God and truly man. He was at one and the same time Lord and man. This helpless baby is Christ the Lord. He is the Lion and the Lamb. He is priest and sacrifice. He who was made weak is strong. He who suffered is made perfect in His suffering.

So we have an admirable conjunction, as well. In Christ, may we know the power of His resurrection. In Christ, may we also know the fellowship of His sufferings and may we continue to learn what it means to take up our cross and follow Him. In Christ, our weakness is made perfect. In Christ, we may be confident.

Chapter Five

CONFIDENCE
IN THE GOSPEL

We see the stability of God's mercy and faithfulness
to His people, how He never forsakes His inheritance, and
remembers His covenant to them through all generations.

—JONATHAN EDWARDS

George Yancey teaches sociology at the University of North Texas. He's a Christian, and he has recently turned his attention to a term that he coined. He studies the changing trends of attitudes of the American population toward Christians and, specifically, theologically conservative Christians. These are Christians who regularly attend church, who affirm the Bible's teaching, and who affirm a set of theologically conservative beliefs. His major research question is this: What do Americans think of these theologically conservative Christians?

The answers he found have led him to coin the term *Christianophobia*. He has reported on his studies in a number of his books. He titled one of them *So Many Christians, So Few Lions*, a line he actually received from a survey respondent. It's an obvious reference to the early centuries of Christianity. As one of the forms of persecution, Christians would be thrown to the lions in the stadium. *So Many Christians, So Few Lions*. Here's a sample of the quotes that he heard during his research:

> The members are generally superstitious, and share the same attitudes that led to the religious atrocities of medieval Europe. . . .
>
> It is to the disgrace of humanity that such ignorance, superstition, and intolerance still persists in the modern age. It is a shame that, in an age of Enlightenment and scientific advancement, pre-medieval superstition is still so evident. . . .
>
> [It] reinforced the idea I had that they were mostly stupid people pushing a program of militant ignorance in the delusionary dream that a magic, invisible, sky-daddy God and his offspring were guiding their every thought and action. . . .
>
> Advanced beyond Santa and the Easter Bunny, but still at a juvenile intellectual stage. . . .
>
> My brother—a highly intelligent but troubled young man—abandoned all reason, and embraced conservative thinking. It is a tremendously depressing waste of his potential.[1]

When we looked at placing our confidence in God's Word in chapter three, we considered the challenges coming from the sciences and the social sciences to Scripture. We saw that many people were finding the Bible to be outmoded, outdated, unhelpful, and even harmful. The views expressed in these quotes share that perspective.

Not only do these views tell us something about the world that we live in, they also raise a significant question: How do we speak the gospel to this kind of a person?

Here's yet another question: Is this kind of a person beyond the pale of the gospel?

Can the gospel still break through to that person who thinks that Christians are a menace and should be thrown to the lions? When we enter a season of conflict, do we only see battle lines drawn? Or do we see our task as proclaiming the gospel and realizing that, even in the face of opposition and hostility, we still have an obligation to preach the gospel even to our enemies?

I raise these questions because I think they help us get to a truly significant question: Do we believe in the power of the gospel?

Stephen Tong is a Chinese-born minister in Indonesia. Islam first entered Indonesia in the thirteenth century and today it stands as the dominant religion. Nearly 90 percent of the population is Muslim. Tong leads the Indonesian Reformed Evangelical Church (*Gereja Reformed Injili Indonesia*, or GRII, in Indonesian), pastors Messiah Cathedral, heads a publishing endeavor, holds evangelistic rallies, composes and conducts music—all with the intent of bringing the light of the gospel to the darkness of Indonesia. He also has something to say to the church in the West. He notices that Christians in the West "always think within our limits." We too often fail to see the power of the gospel.

We see an example of the power of the gospel in Philippians 1. In Philippians, we find ourselves dealing with a biblical author who also happened to be in jail. Paul was in Rome and enduring the first of his two Roman imprisonments. He was released shortly after he wrote Philippians. Then he was rearrested. Then, as church tradition informs, he was martyred, as was Peter, sometime in AD 66 or 67.

Both imprisonments occurred during the reign of Nero. You would be hard pressed to identify a ruler more sinister, more evil than Nero. Historians estimate that thousands, if not tens of thousands, of slaves died in the building of his gardens. Nero's demands were so intense that the sheer workload took their lives. He relentlessly pursued his wicked pleasures. The fact that a number of New Testament books were written during his reign—and that they call Christians to obey the government and honor rulers—tells us a great deal of how to live in hostile territory.

The fact that Nero reigned while Paul wrote Philippians offers significant depth to some of the things Paul writes in this book. At the very end of the book, Paul writes, "All the saints greet you, especially those of Caesar's household" (4:22). The gospel made it all the way into the household of Nero, perhaps history's most notoriously wicked ruler.

We also need to notice the power of the gospel in Philippians 1:12–14:

I want you to know, brothers, that what has happened to me has really served to advance the gospel, so that it has become known throughout the whole imperial guard and to all the rest that my imprisonment is for Christ. And most of the brothers, having become confident in the Lord by my imprisonment, are much more bold to speak the word without fear.

If you were looking for a symbol of Roman power, you could do no better than the Praetorian Guard. These were the elite forces of the Roman army, the trained of the trained. These were the Green Berets, the Army Rangers, the Navy SEALs of their day. The Praetorian Guard was originally established as the protection detail for the Caesars. Over time, their work expanded to including guarding court officials, senators, and Roman officials stationed across the empire. Over the centuries, the Praetorian Guard accumulated significant power and wealth. They rose to such power by the first century that even the Caesars feared them. The Praetorian Guard had the wealth, the immense number of troops, and clearly the skills to launch a military coup d'état.

The qualifications to become a Praetorian guard were high. Consider the sheer physicality and strength, the power and skill one had to have to possess to wear that uniform. Praetorian guards would be at the very peak of physical condition. This force was not merely a symbol of Roman power. In the first century AD, the Praetorian Guard represented the reality of Roman power. These were the men who were Paul's guards. And the gospel made its way into their ranks.

Praetorian guards were routinely shipped around the Roman Empire, serving tours in various places and then getting reassigned to Rome. Paul appreciated this practice, as it meant he would regularly be assigned new guards. His first imprisonment, from what we can reconstruct, did not last long. But thanks to the rotation of his guard, he was able to spread the gospel in what was easily one of the unlikeliest of places in the Roman Empire.

During the decades of the writing of the New Testament and during the centuries of persecution experienced by the early church, the Praetorian Guard would arrest and guard Christians. Now, in Rome in AD 62, Paul was evangelizing them. Paul informs us that his imprisonment "has become known throughout the whole imperial guard." The guards were talking about Paul. They would be guarding him, and then they would get reassigned. On their new assignment, they told their colleagues about their very peculiar prisoner. The word spread. The gospel spread.

Can you imagine when the epistle to the Philippians was first read to the Christians gathered in that city? The word would have spread among them that a letter from Paul had arrived. Then the next Lord's Day would come. Christians likely met throughout the city of Philippi in house churches or in synagogues. On this occasion, perhaps they found a place where they all could gather and hear the letter. One of the pastors would stand, or perhaps the messenger Paul had dispatched to deliver the letter would stand, and read the epistle from Paul to the church at Philippi. How encouraging would these words have been to the Christians who lived there?

One of the Philippian believers in particular would likely have especially enjoyed hearing about the gospel's being declared and being made known among the prison guards. The Philippian jailer from Acts 16:25–31 knew firsthand how persuasive Paul could be with jailers.

Paul wanted the Philippians to know that his imprisonment was not a setback, nor a roadblock, nor a signal of the end of Christianity. Paul's imprisonment was not a sign of the impotence of Christianity in the face of the power of Rome. Rather, Paul's imprisonment signaled the exact opposite. Paul's imprisonment served to advance the gospel. That is the power of the gospel. The letter Paul wrote and the testimony he gave were fully intended to encourage the Philippians to place their confidence in the gospel.

Paul drives this point home further by speaking of the Christians at Rome. After Paul speaks of the gospel's becoming known among the imperial guard, he declares that the Christians in Rome "have become confident in the Lord." That confidence has led them to be "much more bold to speak the Word without fear."

Let's not forget the cultural moment here. They were boldly speaking the gospel in the city of Rome, *in Nero's Rome*. In Nero's day, the grand Circus Maximus grew to its greatest capacity: 250,000 spectators. To this day, it is the largest sporting arena ever. The main event in the Circus was the chariot race. Chariots pulled by four to twelve horses raced for honor and large cash prizes. The track was purposely constructed with sharp turns to promote accidents for the bloodthirsty crowd. Carnage involving horses and charioteers was the norm. The crowds were so raucous that schools closed for a radius of twenty or so miles because the noise drowned everything out. Nero's Rome indulged in barbaric forms of entertainment.

Nero's Rome also indulged in the basest of sexual activities. Roman historians record details of Nero's own sexual exploits, many so gross and heinous that they simply cannot be repeated here. Brothels and sex slaves were the norm. The great Rome was barbaric.

Yet, in the midst of it all, Paul boldly preached the gospel, and the gospel flourished. In what may very well be the theme verses for the epistle to the Romans, Paul declares, "For I am not ashamed of the gospel, for it is the power of God for salvation" (Rom. 1:16). The gospel is the power of God—it will succeed against all odds and against all opposition.

What we see in Philippians 1 is an ever-widening circle of the gospel. Paul boldly proclaims the gospel. The Christians in Rome, inspired by his example, boldly proclaim the gospel. Paul holds out their example to the Philippians to be more bold in proclaiming the gospel. And whom would the Philippian believers inspire? Through the centuries, Christians have read of these examples in these verses and in their corners of the world where they preach the gospel. This is an ever-widening circle.

We started looking at Philippians 1 through the lens of a question. That question is: Do we believe in the power of the gospel? Paul did, and that belief permeated his life. One of the reasons Paul believed in the power of the gospel had to do with his own story. Paul recalls his own story in Philippians 3. Two times in this chapter, Paul uses the phrase "confidence in the flesh." Paul lets us know that he had many reasons to put confidence in his flesh. He had the pedigree. He had the training. He had the drive and determination.

Paul was likely one of the most intelligent people to have ever lived. He certainly is one of the best writers. He was extremely ambitious. He knew adversity, yet he persevered. If anyone "thinks he has reason for confidence in the flesh," Paul tells us, "I have more" (3:4).

Yet, Paul realizes that "whatever gain I had, I counted as loss for the sake of Christ" (3:7). He counts all his accomplishments, all his strivings after righteousness, as "rubbish," a polite word for "dung." All of Paul's abilities and accomplishments simply serve to underscore his utter inability to achieve righteousness.

Instead of putting his confidence in the flesh, Paul learned to put his confidence in Christ and in the gospel. Paul wanted to be found in Christ. He writes, "That I may gain Christ and be found in him, not having a righteousness of my own, but that which comes through faith in Christ, the righteousness from God that depends on faith" (3:9). The theologian Francis Turretin expresses it this way:

> God grant that, dismissing a vain confidence in our own merit, we may rest in the most perfect merit of Christ alone and so keep faithful in him and fight the good fight even unto the end that we might receive the crown of righteousness; due not to our merit, but most graciously promised to us from the heavenly rewarder.[2]

Johnny Cash wrote a novel on the life of the Apostle Paul. Yes, one of country music's icons and one of American music's legends wrote a biography of Paul. Cash called it *The Man in White*, and it is a piece of genius.[3] The "man in white" is actually not Paul. It's Christ. Therein lies Cash's genius. Similarly, Augustine is not the main character in his autobiographical *Confessions*. God is. Paul is not the main character in Cash's biography. He's the prominent and predominant character as the pages unfold. But all along, we get the sense that there is far more to the story than what we are seeing on the page. Behind the scenes of Paul's life, there is one at work, orchestrating all the details to one desired end and one certain outcome.

Paul knew he had to put his confidence in the gospel, because nothing else can turn the human heart and nothing else solves the human dilemma. People think the human dilemma is many things. Some say it's poverty or the unjust distribution of resources and wealth. Some say it's war and our penchant for war. Some simply think the human dilemma is internal and psychological. As R.C. Sproul has often said, "The human dilemma is this: God is holy, and we are not. God is righteous, and we are not." Our problem is not lack or abundance of wealth or resources. Our problem is not that we are a few degrees short of finding utopia. Our problem is the wrath of holy God. No amount of righteousness can solve that dilemma. Paul testifies to only one solution: the righteousness that comes through faith in Christ.

When we think of Luther's main doctrine, we think of justification by faith alone. That doctrine hinges upon one word.

In fact, the entire Reformation and the protest the Reformers launched against the Roman Catholic Church could very well be summed up in this one word: *imputation*. The doctrine of imputation teaches that our sin, which cuts us off and alienates us from a holy God, gets imputed to Christ. Christ paid the penalty for our sin, and so our sins are forgiven. The doctrine of imputation also teaches that Christ's righteousness gets imputed to us. If Christ's work only accomplished the forgiveness of sins, we would be right back to where we were in the garden before Adam and Eve ate of the fruit of the Tree of Knowledge of Good and Evil.

Christ's work overcame the curse and restored "Paradise lost." Christ's work also led to "Paradise regained." We now stand in the very presence of God clothed in Christ's righteousness. The "Man in white" took our filthy rags and gave us His white, pure, and righteous robe. Paul says it plainly in 2 Corinthians 5:21: "He who knew no sin became sin for us that we might become the righteousness of God."

Theologians refer to Christ's work in terms of His *active obedience* and His *passive obedience*. In His passive obedience, He paid the penalty for sin; He atoned for sin. In His active righteousness, He earned righteousness on our behalf. No other message and no other means can save us or deliver us. Paul spent decades and piled effort upon effort in attempts to white-knuckle his way to God. All to no avail. Then, on the road to Damascus, Saul came to an end as Christ, "the Man in white," brought Paul to Himself.

Paul knew firsthand the power of the gospel. Not a day went by that he did not rejoice in what God had done for him in Christ.

The brothers John and Charles Wesley tried white-knuck-ling their way into heaven. They even went to a faraway land as missionaries in a futile attempt to achieve salvation. Then, independently but within a few days of each other, John and Charles were brought to Christ. John was convicted as he stood outside the Aldersgate Meetinghouse in London and heard Martin Luther's preface to his commentary on Romans being read. Charles was convicted as he was reading Martin Luther's preface to his commentary on Galatians. They decided they would no longer celebrate or mark their earthly birthdays. Instead, they would celebrate the occasion of their conversions.

To mark his first new birth birthday, Charles wrote a hymn, "And Can It Be," a hymn to the mystery and wonder of salvation. In one of the stanzas, he declares:

Long my imprisoned spirit lay,
fast bound in sin and nature's night;
thine eye diffused a quickening ray—
I woke, the dungeon flamed with light;
my chains fell off, my heart was free,
I rose, went forth, and followed Thee.

Jessica Buchanan was an aid worker in the lawless lands of Somalia. She worked with a Danish charity, teaching children how to avoid landmines. In October 2011, she was kidnapped by a band of Somali pirates armed with AK-47s. She was held for ninety-three days in the wide open, through the rainy season. Over that time, she became malnourished and began to suffer greatly from a kidney infection. Her captors kept her alive, but barely. Negotiations were stalled. She had lost all hope. In the middle of the night on January 25, 2012, she woke to a sudden and violent eruption of gunfire. She thought a rival gang had engaged her captors in a battle. She buried her head in her hands, thinking she would surely die. Then she felt a hand on her shoulder and heard someone call her name—"*Jessica.*" And she heard it in an American accent.

Under the cover of night, a detachment from U.S. Navy SEAL Team Six parachuted in and attacked the camp. All of the pirates were killed. Jessica was unharmed. The sailors picked her up and carried her out of the camp and to the designated pickup zone. The SEALs then made a circle around her and waited until the helicopter arrived. They loaded her onto the helicopter and she was carried off to safety. As the helicopter lifted off, one of the SEALs handed her an American flag.

Jessica Buchanan contributed nothing to her release from her captors. The SEALs did it all. And when they rescued her, literally from the pit of death, they gave her back her identity. They gave her back her freedom.

Her story is a picture of this stanza from Charles Wesley's hymn. It is a hymn commemorating a prison break. The prisoner could no nothing. This prison break was only possible through the work of Christ. So Charles Wesley's hymn declares:

> Jesus, and all in Him, is mine;
> alive in Him, my living Head,
> and clothed in righteousness divine.

The quickening ray is able to penetrate the darkest of dungeons. It penetrated the Praetorian Guard and even the household of Nero.

In the middle of July 64, Rome burned. Nero likely caused the fire. He had ambitious plans to rebuild Rome, but there were current buildings in his way. The belief of historians is that Nero's underlings set the fire to help speed along his revitalization plans. The fire, however, spread out of control. It burned for a week and may have consumed as much as 70 percent of the city.

Fingers started pointing at Nero. The Roman historian Tacitus tells us that to shift the blame off of himself, Nero fixed the blame on Christians. An intense season of persecution ensued. Tacitus further informs us that Nero used Christians as living torches to illumine his gardens at night so he could be entertained by chariot races. Nero's cruelty knew no bounds.

The persecution he unleashed lasted until the end of his reign in AD 68. Sometime between 64 and 68, Nero handed down the order for Paul to be rearrested and for Peter to be arrested. Both were executed before Nero's death. This is the cultural backdrop for the growth of the church and for the New Testament writings.

Rome had two designations for the religions it encountered across its spreading empire. One of those designations was *religio licita*, which means "legal religion." The other was *superstitio illicita*, which means "illegal superstition." The word *superstition* reveals how contemptuous Rome found these practices to be. As Rome overtook other peoples, for the most part those people groups were polytheists. This presented no problems to Rome. This simply meant more gods to add to the Roman pantheon. Most of the religions that came into the empire were dubbed *religio licita*. They had the stamp of approval of Rome and could be practiced freely. Judaism was granted *religio licita* status primarily because Jews didn't tend to proselytize a great deal. But from its beginnings, Christianity was designated a *superstitio illicita*.

As a consequence, Christians were literally enemies of the state—marginalized, ostracized, and persecuted. They could be killed with impunity. To be a Christian was to identify with a group of people who were worthy of nothing but shame and scorn. To the best Romans, Christians were seen as worthy of sympathy for their primitive ways. To the worst Romans, the death of Christians could provide entertainment. Ridding Christians from the empire would be the best possible outcome.

Tacitus refers to Christianity with the designation *superstitio illicita* and testifies to the hatred the Roman populace had for Christians. This despite the fact that Christians in these early centuries lived exemplary lives. Early apologists such as Athenagoras and Justin Martyr testify to the lives Christians lived. They promoted virtue. They honored the emperor. They had a work ethic that set them apart. Paul admonished servants to work "as for the Lord" (Col. 3:23). Christians had loving families that showed genuine concern for each other. Yet, they were seen to be a criminal element and enemies of the state. They were hated—not because of their behavior, for their behavior was laudatory. If only all Romans lived like the Christians. They were hated for their beliefs. They were hated for their belief in Christ and in the gospel. Ultimately, Christians were hated because their beliefs were different, and their beliefs challenged the status quo.

Christus, their leader, was hated also, and He was killed on a cross under Pontius Pilate. His followers were all guilty—simply for being Christians. In the midst of all of this, we have Paul's testimony in Philippians to the power of the gospel.

There is power in the gospel. And there is every reason for us to put our confidence in the gospel. In fact, we're obligated to. We're obligated to proclaim this Word.

Good News

Like Paul, Peter also knew firsthand the power of the gospel. This burly fisherman, who could be coarse, rude, and rough, talks about sincere and pure love. In fact, he commands such a love. He commands us to "love one another earnestly from a pure heart" (1 Peter 1:22). We all want such a love to be the reality in our lives and relationships. We want this for our families, for our churches, and for our circles of friends. Peter not only commands such a love, he tells us how such love is possible. It is possible because we have been born again. We are new creatures. It is also possible because we have been born again by the true, the living, and the abiding Word of God. Everything else fades and falls away. God's pure Word alone abides.

That God's Word abides forever reminds us that other things change. Laws change. Social mores and values change. Even

societies change. Empires and nations
Word abides forever. Psalm 110:160 decl.
word is truth, and every one of your righ
forever." This is the same abiding Word that
his epistle.

To make his point, Peter quotes Isaiah:

> All flesh is like grass
> and all its glory like the flower of grass.
> The grass withers,
> and the flower falls,
> but the word of the Lord remains forever. (1 Peter 1:24)

The quote comes from Isaiah 40. That chapter is a message of comfort, as we saw in chapter two. A voice is crying out, not of judgment, but of rescue, deliverance, and salvation. Peter quotes from Isaiah 40:6–8. But he is also thinking of what comes next. Right after his quote, Peter declares, "And this is the good news that was preached to you" (1 Peter 1:25). Back in Isaiah 40:9, right after the quoted material, we read this: "Go up to a high mountain, O Zion, herald of good news."

We already established in chapter two that heralds herald. Heralds declared news, sometimes good and sometimes bad. They were an official position. They were respected and depended upon by the people they served. When Peter thinks of the living and abiding Word of God, he is thinking of its power and efficacy. He thinks of it as the good news of the gospel.

The word *gospel* in the original Greek is a compound word

rally means "good news." *Euangelion* is the word. The
prefix *eu* means "good," and the word *angelos* means "message." We get the English word *angel*, a messenger, from this
Greek word. When William Tyndale translated this word in his
English Bible, he used the phrase "glad tidings."

We see the power of the gospel, the good news, in Isaiah
40:9–11:

> Go on up to a high mountain,
>> O Zion, herald of good news;
> lift up your voice with strength,
>> O Jerusalem, herald of good news;
>> lift it up, fear not;
> say to the cities of Judah,
>> "Behold your God!"
> Behold, the Lord GOD comes with might,
>> and his arm rules for him;
> behold, his reward is with him,
>> and his recompense before him.
> He will tend his flock like a shepherd;
>> he will gather the lambs in his arms;
> he will carry them in his bosom,
>> and gently lead those that are with young.

The prophet pointed the people of Israel away from their
captivity. The prophet pointed the people of Israel away from
the might of Babylon and the sheer force of Medo-Persia, of
Nebuchadnezzar, and later Cyrus. The prophet pointed directly

to God: "Behold your God!" God will unleash vengeance on His enemies. At the same time, God will carry His children all the way home. Yes, Zion, this is good news.

So Peter remembered. He remembered when Andrew, his brother, first took him to see the Messiah. He remembered when he confessed that Jesus is the Christ, the Son of the living God, and Jesus called him blessed. He remembered vowing never to forsake Christ. He remembered the dark hour when he did deny Him. He remembered that Jesus said to him, "Simon, Simon . . . I have prayed for you." He remembered the cross, the empty tomb, and the risen Savior. Just like Paul, Peter knew firsthand the power of the gospel. It was the good news that was preached to him.

Consider again Peter's words to close out the first chapter of his first epistle. Why does he say, "This is the good news that was preached to you"? Is it that he wants them to remember? I think that is part of it. We can have the earnest and sincere love. We can live holy lives. As Peter also commands, we can stand firm in our faith—even in the direst of circumstances—because of the gospel. We must remember the gospel.

But I think there's more. Peter does not want us to be selfish with the gospel. The good news was preached to us—are we not grateful? Are we not grateful that someone preached the good news of the gospel to us? How can we not preach it to others also? Our reluctance or spotty record of preaching the gospel might be owing to the idea that we have forgotten that it is the good news. Or maybe we think, very wrongly, that people do not need it. Or maybe we fear rejection by those who reject the gospel. Maybe we fear hostile responses. None of these, however, has legitimacy. None of these should keep us from heralding glad tidings.

So much that we hear and see is bad news. Depressing news. This good news of the gospel lifts our hearts and causes our souls to sing. We need to hear it. But we must never be selfish with the good news of the gospel.

We need to get up on a high mountain and raise our voices. Like Isaiah, we need to herald to a world distracted and distressed and say, "Behold your God!" In fact, we can be like another prophet, one in the wilderness who pointed to Christ and said, "Behold the Lamb of God, who takes away the sin of the world" (John 1:29). This is the beauty of the gospel. Jesus is the Lamb.

We are all heralds of good news. Or, at least, we should be. And we must never forget how much we ourselves need to hear and remember anew the good news.

Eaten by Moths

In 1739, Jonathan Edwards preached a series of thirty sermons from one verse in Isaiah. Yes, thirty sermons on one verse. The verse was Isaiah 51:8. In the previous verse, we read:

> Listen to me, you who know righteousness,
>   the people in whose heart is my law;
> fear not the reproach of man,
>   nor be dismayed at their revilings.

We need not fear or quake in the face of opposition and adversity. God's people have an immunity, ultimate immunity, from persecution. We simply need the right perspective, the perspective of the gospel. And so, in the text Edwards chose to give a tour-de-force overview of the "History of the Work of Redemption," we hear these words:

> For the moth will eat them up like a garment,
>   and the worm will eat them like wool;
> but my righteousness will be forever,
>   and my salvation to all generations.

Appearances throw us off. They cause us to stumble. They cause us to falter and cower. We forget how temporary the things of this world truly are. We forget how tenuous the enemies of God are. They will pass like a garment. I distinctly remember one sad moment at a garage sale. I pulled my car off the road on to the grass and stepped out to hunt for some hidden treasure. There was a box with some World War II memorabilia lying on top. I showed some interest and quickly the seller came up to me. He told me that inside the box were his father's uniforms. We carefully removed the top only to find the worn and threadbare elements that once made up a proud war hero's uniform.

There is one singular reality that endures. Edwards introduced this sermon series with these words:

> The drift of this chapter [Isaiah 51] is to comfort the church under her sufferings and the persecution of her enemies. And the argument of consolation insisted

upon is the constancy and perpetuity of God's mercy and faithfulness towards her, which shall be manifest in the continuance of the fruits of that mercy and faithfulness in continuing to work salvation for her, protecting her against all assaults of her enemies, and carrying her safely through all the changes of the world and finally crowning her with victory and deliverance.[4]

This is a deeply poignant and pastoral paragraph. These words were first preached in March 1739. They could be preached right now. We are currently experiencing significant "changes of the world." We are in need of consolation and comfort, courage and confidence. Edwards declares that he will insist upon one message that can deliver such consolation: the faithfulness of God's mercy, manifest and demonstrated in the fixed and firm work of salvation. This is comfort and joy now, and it will be even more so in the age to come.

In the course of the sermons, Edwards references Islam. He was curious about the spread of Islam, and he tried to learn as much about it as he could. At one point in the sermon series, Edwards offers a run-through of the history of Islam from its beginnings through the sixteenth century, carefully noting "the church was upheld during this dark day."[5] Edwards also encourages his congregation by reminding them at the final judgment, Islam will be "utterly overthrown."

In the sermon series, Edwards also speaks of the Antichrist, he speaks of heathenism, he speaks of hedonism. Edwards notes how these enemies seem strong and invincible, ever marching on. He acknowledges how things as they appear can be discouraging. Yet, he recognizes the sovereignty of God over all the earth and recognizes that God is working all things to bring about the purpose and plan of redemption. So, with confidence in the gospel, and with joy and pleasure in the gospel, we trust in God knowing that He wins.

In the first of the thirty sermons on Isaiah 51:8, Edwards declares that there is one "sum of all those works of God." There is one chief work that defines and centers all of human history. It is God's work of salvation. History is the history of redemption. It is the grand narrative that shapes all of life and meaning. Redemption is the center, guiding and governing the details. There is not chaos; there is nothing random. God has bent His bow, He has taken aim, and the arrow of His purposes and intentions will hit squarely on the mark.

Not only does redemption give shape and meaning to human history, redemption gives shape and meaning to individual lives. The movie playing out on the big screen has not been left to chance. God governs history and moves it along toward His desired end and purpose as surely as the sun rises. The short clip, playing out on the small screen, has not been left to chance, either. God's purposes for His people, the individual purposes for His individual people, will come to pass. We can have confidence in God's work of redemption.

Near the very end of the sermon series, Edwards concludes:

> Let us with like pleasure and joy celebrate the everlasting duration of God's mercy and faithfulness to his

church and people. And let us be comforted by it during the present dark circumstances that the church of God is under, and all the uproar and confusion there is in the world, and all the threatenings of the church's enemies. And let us take encouragement earnestly to pray for those glorious things which God has promised to accomplish for the church.[6]

Paul defines the gospel for his readers in Ephesians 3:1–14. This densely packed text, which is one long and glorious sentence in the Greek, offers any number of encouraging and comforting ideas—all of which serve to bolster our confidence in the gospel and in the God of the gospel. Three things stand out. First, the gospel and God's plan of redemption unite all things and restore all things. All the broken pieces, all the disjointed fragments are restored and united. The gospel brings restoration and wholeness to the fractured heap.

Second, the gospel is our inheritance. We enjoy so many things now—forgiveness of sins; freedom in Christ; fellowship with the triune God; fellowship with one another; purpose, meaning, and direction in life; the assurance of the Holy Spirit. We enjoy so many things now, but these are but a down payment of the life to come and of the full inheritance that awaits God's children. Not only is the gospel our inheritance, but we are sealed. There is absolute certainty here. We are guaranteed delivery. The Holy Spirit is our seal.

Third, Ephesians 1:3–14 teaches us that the gospel is to the praise of the glory of God's grace. Three times we are told in this passage that salvation is to the praise of God. The gospel leads us to worship. It has been said that theology leads to doxology. Theology leads to worship. We were made to worship God, to glorify Him, to sing His praises. There is an eternal chorus of praise resounding right now in the heavens, while we sing the song of redemption and praise on earth. Someday, we will join the heavenly chorus.

It is fitting that B.B. Warfield said, "The words of Ephesians 1:3–14 should never be read. They should be sung." May we put our confidence in the song of the gospel.

Blessed be the God and Father of our Lord Jesus Christ, who has blessed us in Christ with every spiritual blessing in the heavenly places, even as he chose us in him before the foundation of the world, that we should be holy and blameless before him. In love he predestined us for adoption as sons through Jesus Christ, according to the purpose of his will, to the praise of his glorious grace, with which he has blessed us in the Beloved. In him we have redemption through his blood, the forgiveness of our trespasses, according to the riches of his grace, which he lavished upon us, in all wisdom and insight making known to us the mystery of his will, according to his purpose, which he set forth in Christ as a plan for the fullness of time, to unite all things in him, things in heaven and things on earth.

In him we have obtained an inheritance, having been predestined according to the purpose of him who works all things according to the counsel of his will, so that we who were the first to hope in Christ might be to the praise of his glory. In him you also, when you heard the word of truth, the gospel of your salvation, and believed in him, were sealed with the promised Holy Spirit, who is the guarantee of our inheritance until we acquire possession of it, to the praise of his glory. (Eph. 1:3–14)

Chapter Six

CONFIDENCE
IN HOPE

We have great things in hand, but greater things in hope.

—JEREMIAH BURROUGHS

The life of believers is totally sustained
and guided by hope.

—HERMAN BAVINCK

t could be confidence in love. The poet Virgil declared, "*Amor vincit omnia*," love conquers all. Paul said "the greatest of these is love" (1 Cor. 13:13). Jesus asked Peter three times, "Do you love me?" Was that Peter's final preparation for his becoming a leader of the church? Was that all it took for Peter to stand firm in his Roman cell? Maybe those words echoed in his ears as he was marched to his martyrdom. We could easily speak of confidence in love.

Though it sounds incongruous at first, we could speak of confidence in humility. Humility, of course, has nothing to do with being downtrodden, weak, and going through life with an ever-ready apology merely for taking up space. Humility is the recognition of that all-important theological fact of who God is and who we are. It is a recognition of our dependence. Humility leads Paul to urge his readers to take no confidence in the flesh (Phil. 3:4). Humility is not a barrier to confidence, not a hindrance. Instead, humility is essential to a proper confidence.

Confidence in numbers works too. For far too long, we have suffered, especially in the Western church, from the cultural ideal of rugged individualism. The lone hero is the stuff of comic books and movies, but not what you find in the pages of the New Testament. Time and again, Scripture admonishes us concerning our life together. The "one anothers" of the Bible remind us how mutually dependent we are. Those commands remind us that our care for one another is both a high privilege and a holy obligation. We must intercede for one another in prayer and in good works. We are in this together, and in the body of Christ, the church, we have confidence.

Confidence in prayer should not be overlooked. The author of Hebrews tells us we can go before the very throne of God in confidence (Heb. 4:16). Boldness. How weak and feeble our prayers are, how small. Is there a bolder prayer than "Thy kingdom come, Thy will be done"? We can pray for God's will to be accomplished in our lives, in our families, and in our churches. We can pray for God's will to be accomplished in our communities and in our nations. And we can pray with confidence, because all of God's purposes and plans will be accomplished. We likely do not pray *in confidence* enough.

But while we live on earth and await God's will, which is forever settled in heaven, to come to full fruition, we hope. While we see Christ reigning as King now, seated on the heavenly throne at the Father's right hand, we await the full manifestation and revelation of His glorious kingdom. It will be glorious. The sheer luminosity of the triune God will put the sun and the stars, even entire galaxies, to shame. There will be no comparison. The Lamb slain before the foundation of the world will be there. The Lamb will be in the center and the kings of the earth will bring in their glory, and we will reign with Him forever. It will be glorious.

Jonathan Edwards spoke of the redeemed as finally being "unclogged" in heaven. The Father lavished His love upon the Son. Out of love, the Father sent the Son for us. Pure love flows within the triune Godhead. In Christ, God pours out that love upon us. We then love God and love each other. Yet, now we love so weakly. We are, as Edwards tells us, clogged by sin. In heaven, we are unclogged. As Edwards declared, "Heaven is a world of love."[1]

So we have hope. We long for the day of the fulfillment of all God's promises. But now we live in between. We live in between the promise and the fulfillment. Four hundred silent years passed between the last oracle given by God through the prophet Malachi and the birth of Christ. Simeon routinely went to the temple. Every day, he left his home, walked the route, entered the temple, and waited. He believed that he would see the promised Messiah. When he was an old man, near death, he looked upon the infant born to the Virgin Mary.

Not all hope breeds confidence. Some hopes get dashed, some get destroyed, and some never deliver. There can be such a thing as a false hope, which leads to a false confidence, which sadly disappoints and defeats.

Some have referred to the twentieth century as the century of disillusionment. It launched, however, with a tremendous optimism. Great progress was occurring on all fronts. Then came the devastation of World War I, and then the economic collapse in Europe as inflation soared and in America as the stock market plunged. Then came World War II. In addition to Hitler and Mussolini, dictators and mass murderers plagued other parts of the world. It was a century of genocides. The promise of communism held many in its grasp. Then it collapsed.

Edith Wharton called her novel, set in the late nineteenth century, *The Age of Innocence*. As the twentieth century appeared on the horizon, optimism and innocence persisted. Then came the 1910s and the Great War, and then the 1920s and 1930s and the economic collapse, followed by another decade visited by war. The innocence was shattered. Existentialism and nihilism—the reigning philosophical schools in Europe during the second half of the twentieth century—testify to the death of the optimism that accompanied the beginning of the twentieth century. The philosophers in these schools sounded like prophets of doom.

In one sense, these philosophers are prophets. They stood at the transition from modernity—and its abiding and unshakable belief in progress—to postmodernity. Postmodernity has been defined and described in many ways. Perhaps the best way to get a handle on it is to see it as the end or the demise of all that modernity stood for and all that modernity held to be true. Modernity believed in progress brought about through the pursuit of pure knowledge by means of the scientific method. This fundamentally pitted modernity against religion and faith—a fissure that went back to Immanuel Kant. As we saw in chapter three, the question going into the twentieth century was this: Is the Bible our authority or is science? Modernity put its hope in science.

Modernity fostered a nearly messianic view of institutions. This is seen most poignantly and tragically in the fascist governments of the twentieth century, in the experiments in socialism and communism, and in the experiments in big government. Modernity put its hope in institutions. Fundamentally, modernity put its hope in man. God was continually shoved to the margins, leaving only room for the creation and creatures. *We must hope in ourselves*, said the voices of modernity.

Against all of these "messiahs" of modernity, postmodernity responds with one word: suspicion. The postmodernist likes Elvis: "We can't go on like this with suspicious minds." So postmodernity sees the flaws and the cracks in modernity. The peculiar thing, however, is that the postmodern ethos seems rather satisfied without having an alternative.

In the history of ideas, new ideas came along that challenged old ones. New ideas presented themselves as having better answers. Postmodernity thinks modernity's answers are wrong. It does not, however, rush in to the vacuum with new ideas.

I was wrong. Postmoderns actually don't like Elvis. They *do* want to go on like this with suspicious minds. Postmodernity has been dubbed a philosophy of despair. Disappointment breeds cynicism, which breeds disillusionment, which breeds despair. All of this crowds out hope.

Modernity eventually collapsed, but not because of the critique by postmodernity. It collapsed because it held to a view of the world that is false. It collapsed of its own accord. Postmodernism too is untenable and either has already collapsed or will collapse. Not because a new perspective will come along to refute it, but because of a plain fact: postmodernity is a false view of the world. Postmodernity does not cohere, and eventually it will collapse.

What does all of this talk of the coming and going of ideas mean? It means this, both in the twentieth and in the twenty-first centuries: The prevailing worldviews did not and cannot offer real answers. Modernity says, "Hope in man." That doesn't work. Postmodernity says, "Abandon hope." That doesn't work either.

Humanity cannot live without hope.

The Things Hoped For

Remo Giazotto, a composer and musician, claimed to have found a never-before-known piece of music by the eighteenth-century composer Tomaso Albinoni in the rubble of Dresden, Germany. It's an adagio, meaning it's slow, at ease. *Adagio* is a musical notation that directs musicians to slow down the tempo. Consequently, adagios are peaceful and restful. "Albinoni's Adagio" is also beautiful. To think that such a piece of beauty could be found amid the rubble of destruction—it is almost enough to restore hope, to restore one's faith in humanity. It is enough to give one hope to rebuild, hope to think the horrors of the war would not be repeated.

But it's a false hope. The music is beautiful, but there's simply no evidence that it was a discovery of a lost piece of music. What Giazotto's intentions were in telling the story, we'll never know. In all likelihood, Giazotto composed the piece himself. There is something about the human spirit that wants to find hope, that wants to somehow pull hope out of the rubble, even if that hope has to be invented.

The hope in Scripture, the hope that gives us confidence, is not something we have to create or prop up. Biblical hope is a sure thing.

John's "beatific vision" in 1 John 3:1–3 offers an example of the absolute certainty regarding our hope. Here, John tells us:

> See what kind of love the Father has given to us, that we should be called children of God; and so we are. The reason why the world does not know us is that it did not know him. Beloved, we are God's children now, and what we will be has not yet appeared; but we know that when he appears we shall be like him, because we shall see him as he is. And everyone who thus hopes in him purifies himself as he is pure.

John begins with his inability to describe fully and truly the love of God for His children. John simply invites us to see the depth of the Father's love in that God has sent His Son. John invites us to see that through our union with Christ, we are adopted into the family of God. We are His children.

John offers us here a rather fascinating look at the verb *to be*. We see here what we were, what we are, and what we will be.

Our past identity, what we were, is an implication in this text. We were not always children of God. Paul tells us we were "children of wrath" (Eph. 2:2). We were alienated from God. It's a lie, and a terrible one at that, to think that we were neutral or, worse, born good. Augustine called humanity "Adam's sinful lump." We were not good; we were not even neutral. We were born sinners, and as such, we were repugnant to the holy God. We could not stand in His presence for even a nanosecond. The prophet Isaiah immediately dropped to the ground when he had his encounter with God, who was declared three-times holy. Isaiah was undone, as if someone had simply pulled on a loose thread of a large tapestry and the whole thing unraveled into a pile of yarn. As R.C. Sproul writes in his classic text *The Holiness of God*, "To be undone means to come apart at the seams, to be unraveled. What Isaiah was expressing is what modern psychologists describe as the experience of personal disintegration." When Isaiah was measured against the standard of God's holiness, "he was destroyed—morally and spiritually annihilated."[2]

We need to start with who we were. Only when we come to grips with who we were can we fully appreciate what we are and fully appreciate the work of redemption that transformed us and made us new creatures. When we were the enemies of

God, at that precise time, He saved us. At our conversion to Christ, we have an awareness of our sin. We feel the pangs of the Spirit's convictions. We know of our need for a savior, for Christ alone to atone for our sin and to clothe us with His righteousness. But how little we know of the full ugliness of our sin, our utter unworthiness. How little we know of the holiness of God. How can we fully appreciate the words of those magnificent angelic beings as they circle the throne of heaven and cry out, "Holy, holy, holy is the Lord of hosts"? Throughout our Christian lives, we will continue to grow in our appreciation of the depth of our sin and the towering height of God's holiness.

Part of Christian maturity is realizing more and more who we really and truly were and appreciating more and more who we are now. We have come so far. We have actually come a nearly infinite distance from being children of wrath to being children of God.

Who are we? Two times in as many verses in 1 John 3, we are told that we are children of God. God's love is the only reason given here as to how and why we are the children of God. Two texts from Deuteronomy explain how God's sovereign election is owing to nothing in us. In fact, Deuteronomy 7:6–8 makes the point that Israel was the least of all the nations:

> For you are a people holy to the Lord your God. The Lord your God has chosen you to be a people for his treasured possession, out of all the peoples who are on the face of the earth. It was not because you were more in number than any other people that the Lord set his

love on you and chose you, for you were the fewest of all peoples, but it is because the LORD loves you and is keeping the oath that he swore to your fathers, that the LORD has brought you out with a mighty hand and redeemed you from the house of slavery, from the hand of Pharaoh king of Egypt.

When theologians speak of election, they speak of it as unconditional. There is no condition in us that warrants God's election or forces God's hand. It's the opposite. There is a beautiful tautology here. God set His love on you because He loves you. A few chapters later in Deuteronomy, God ups the ante. Not only do all the nations belong to God, from the vast and mighty to the few and weak, but even the heavens belong to God. Yet again, God chose Israel to be His people. So, Deuteronomy 10:14–15 tells us:

Behold, to the LORD your God belong heaven and the heaven of heavens, the earth with all that is in it. Yet the LORD set his heart in love on your fathers and chose their offspring after them, you above all peoples, as you are this day.

One year after Luther posted his Ninety-Five Theses, he presented an entirely new set of theses in the city of Heidelberg along a tributary of the Rhine River. The Heidelberg Chapter House of the Augustinian Order, Luther's monastic order, hosted a gathering of his fellow monks to hear him out and to weigh his challenge to Rome. He drew a sharp distinction between what he called "theologians of glory" and "theologians of the cross." Theologians of glory stressed human glory, human ability. Theologians of the cross went the opposite direction. The cross shouts "No!" to human ability. The cross points to our inability and our depraved state.

Then Luther writes one of his most insightful sentences in thesis 28: "The love of God does not find, but creates, that which is pleasing to it."[3] How mysterious and marvelous is the love of God. We tend to be fair-weather fans, ducking for cover and nowhere to be found when the foul times come. We look for the lovely or the worthy and then love it. God's love is the opposite. While we were His enemies, He loved us in Christ.

We have been focusing on the love of God. We also need to see God as our Father and see ourselves as His children. A beautiful way to express this is the doctrine of adoption. The Westminster Confession of Faith teaches this concerning the doctrine of adoption:

> All those that are justified, God vouchsafes, in and for His only Son Jesus Christ, to make partakers of the grace of adoption, by which they are taken into the number, and enjoy the liberties and privileges of the children of God, have His name put upon them, receive the spirit of adoption, have access to the throne of grace with boldness, are enabled to cry, Abba, Father, are pitied, protected, provided for, and chastened by Him as by a Father: yet never cast off, but sealed to the day of

redemption; and inherit the promises, as heirs of ever-lasting salvation. (WCF 12.1)

Adoption means more than being sons. Adoption means we are heirs. All that Christ secured is ours. God is our Father. So we have confidence in our identity now, confidence in who we are. We have a firm and fixed confidence in being a child of God.

We also have confidence in our hope of who we shall be. Again, John tells us, "We know that when he appears we shall be like him, because we shall see him as he is."

We will be like Him. Paul teaches us that we are being transformed from one degree of glory to another (2 Cor. 3:12–18). We are being fashioned after the image of Christ. As we mature spiritually, we are undergoing a transformation, a renewal. Someday, we will be transfigured; we will be glorified. Our transformation will be complete. As we mentioned earlier, Jonathan Edwards would add that someday, we will be unclogged. We will fully know; we will fully love. The righteous standing before God, earned for us by the perfect obedience of Christ, will not only be our position, it will be the reality. All our remaining sin will flee like shadows when the lights come on in a room. Our feeble and frail bodies, what Paul calls at one place our "earthly tents," will give way to our glorified bodies (2 Cor. 5:1). All tears will be wiped away. As if it were not enough for John to call us children of God, he now tells us that this, in and through Christ, is what awaits us. This is what we will be.

Someday, we will be like Him. That's the beatific vision. That's the hope. That's the felicity—pure happiness—that Augustine speaks of in the closing pages of *City of God*. That's the world of love spoken of by Jonathan Edwards. When we are free from all of those things that deter and detract from pure worship, we will be fully and finally what God intends for us to be. What we will be is our hope, and that is our confidence.

In 1 John 3:1–3, John actually gives us four takes on the verb *to be* as it relates to our identity. There is who we were, who we are, and who we will be. The fourth is this: who we are becoming.

John tells us in eight significant words: *what we will be has not yet appeared*.

Those words should be emblazoned upon our foreheads. We are not yet what we will be, and all those fellow believers around us are also not yet what they will be. This could be of significant help to us as we encounter those little frictions that come up among each other, those frictions that come up in our churches, and those frictions that come up in our families. This is what parents need to tell themselves every time they look at their kids. *What they will be has not yet appeared.* Teachers need to tell this to themselves regarding their students. Pastors need to remember this concerning the members of their congregation. It helps us to have that necessary and rare commodity of patience with one another.

It can be very comforting and assuring to remember "what we will be has not yet appeared." This phrase also helps us have patience with ourselves.

The Canons of Dort, one of the most rewarding of Reformation texts, comes from the 1610s. This decade witnessed a controversy between the Calvinists and Jacob Arminius and the beginning of Arminianism in the Netherlands. The followers of Arminius drew up a document made up of five heads, or topics, of doctrine called the Remonstrance. These five heads remonstrated, or gave an intense demonstration, against the teachings of John Calvin on the doctrines of grace. This controversy provided the opportunity to summarize Calvin's teaching and to offer a response to its critics. The document written to refute the Remonstrance is known as the Canons of Dort. Canons are church rulings, and Dort, or Dordt, is short for Dordtrecht, the city in the Netherlands that hosted the Dutch Reformed Church synod that addressed the controversy.

Centuries later, the Canons of Dort, which consisted of five heads of articles and rejections that addressed each head of the Remonstrance, was shortened to a five-letter acrostic: TULIP. The *T* stands for total depravity, the *U* for unconditional election, the *L* for limited atonement, the *I* for irresistible grace, and the *P* for perseverance of the saints (or, as some prefer, the preservation of the saints).

It has been my experience that many people know of TULIP, but very few have actually read either the Remonstrance or the Canons of Dort. That is regrettable. There is a key line from the second head of doctrine in the Canons of Dort. The order of the points is actually ULTIP, not TULIP, but ULTIP is not a word. Nevertheless, under the controversial point of *L*, limited atonement, the second head of Dort states:

> For it was the entirely free plan and very gracious will
> and intention of God the Father that the enlivening

and saving effectiveness of his Son's costly death should work itself out in all the elect, in order that God might grant justifying faith to them only and thereby lead them without fail to salvation. In other words, it was God's will that Christ through the blood of the cross (by which he confirmed the new covenant) should effectively redeem from every people, tribe, nation, and language all those and only those who were chosen from eternity to salvation and given to him by the Father; that Christ should grant them faith (which, like the Holy Spirit's other saving gifts, he acquired for them by his death). It was also God's will that Christ should cleanse them by his blood from all their sins, both original and actual, whether committed before or after their coming to faith; that he should faithfully preserve them to the very end; and that he should finally present them to himself, a glorious people, without spot or wrinkle.

This fully packed statement speaks not simply of our conversion but looks straight ahead to our glorification. We are clothed in Christ's righteous robes from the very moment of our salvation. Yet, in this life, we, through our besetting sins and imperfections, wrinkle those garments. Like the spot of red sauce on the white shirt worn to an Italian restaurant, we get spots on our garments. Someday, we will be clothed in pure raiment—no spots, no wrinkles.

If we skip ahead to the last head of Dort, to the *P* of preservation of the saints, we read:

This assurance of perseverance, however, so far from making true believers proud and carnally self-assured, is rather the true root of humility, of childlike respect, of genuine godliness, of endurance in every conflict, of fervent prayers, of steadfastness in crossbearing and in confessing the truth, and of well-founded joy in God. Reflecting on this benefit provides an incentive to a serious and continual practice of thanksgiving and good works, as is evident from the testimonies of Scripture and the examples of the saints.

The assurance of our perseverance serves to fortify us now. We can stand firm and endure all types of hardships because we know what the end of the story will be, and we know that there will be an end of the story. Occasionally, I sign up for a class at the gym. One in particular is brutal. It starts at 10 a.m. and ends at 11 a.m. on Saturdays. While I'm in it, I only have one hope—11 a.m. will come. To use the profound words of Dort, "reflecting on this benefit"—that 11 a.m. will come and I can go home—"provides an incentive." We need the incentive.

Christ endured the cross for the joy that was set before Him (Heb. 12:2). Joy awaits us. Yes, we can endure. Yes, we can do this. We have our incentive.

We are children of God. We will be pure and spotless. In the meantime, what we will be has not yet appeared. It is in the process of appearing as we are in the process of becoming. But we are not there yet.

What we will be has not yet appeared. This in no way

becomes an excuse to condone sin, either in us or in others. But it's a reminder that we are not yet what we will be.

These words also remind us that we are in the process of becoming more like Christ, or at least we should be. What we will be has not yet appeared, but we are on our way. This, too, gives us hope and confidence.

John Newton was a slave trader with a mouth that made even his fellow sailors blush. Then he was converted to Christ. We should not wonder that he gave us that beautiful hymn "Amazing Grace." He also once said something that rather poetically sums up all of this teaching on our identity in 1 John 1:1–3: "I am not what I ought to be, I am not what I want to be, I am not what I hope to be in another world; but still I am not what I once used to be, and by the grace of God I am what I am."

These three verses from 1 John 3 are like a multifaceted diamond that continues to stun as we look into it and turn it over in our minds. John wants us to have hope. A hope for the future, but also a hope that has everything to do with the present. We see this when we ask: What does this hope do?

This hope does not send us into the fortress to pine away for the world to come. It doesn't send us, like Jerome, into a cave. The last time we looked at Jerome, in chapter one, he was hiding out in a cave and waiting for the end of the world. The kind of hope John speaks of here does not send us into a cave to wait it out. Instead, this hope sends us back into the world. What John says here, the application of the beatific vision, is that hope has everything to do with how we live in the world, because whoever has this hope purifies himself even as God is pure (v. 3).

John's call for purity was stunningly countercultural. He may very well have been calling his audience to an apologetic. First-century Rome was not known for its purity. John likely wrote his epistles in the late 80s. In 79, a volcano destroyed Pompeii. What has been preserved from that site testifies to the city's debauchery. We see a similar decadence in our own day. A group of men were arrested in Atlantic City in the 1930s for appearing on the beach without shirts. In 1937, the officials responsible for the beach lifted the requirement of shirts on men. While we need to avoid a nostalgic view of the past, we also can't help but notice that moral standards seem to be in a freefall in our time.

God's Word commands us to be pure, and this is not according to a sliding scale. The standard for purity is God Himself. Peter tells us to be holy as God is holy. John tells us to be pure as God is pure. The standard used here puts a full stop on any flirtation with moral relativism. We must not lament the moral decline of our age only to become coconspirators ourselves in subtle ways. We must be pure. All the more, John wants to say to his audience, given the culture of his day. All the more for us, too, given the moral decline of our day. Though some took issue with him, and with the particular arguments of his book, Robert Bork's book title from 1993 perhaps rings more true today: *Slouching towards Gomorrah.*

In this cultural and moral decline, with humble and contrite hearts, we ask if we have slackened in our obedience to John's command to be pure. Have we succumbed to the cultural confusion? In a time when everything's up for grabs and in a place where no principles seem to govern moral decisions and judgments, we must be careful that we do not slowly succumb and start, inch by inch, slouching ourselves.

This honest and humble self-searching and self-awareness will help keep us from a posture of self-righteousness and moral superiority. It will also help us think of our apologetic stance as a people of purity. It would be a potent testimony to the power of the gospel simply to be a people of purity in this world.

Why would John single out purity? John could just as easily have said, "Everyone who has this hope is full of joy." To be a person of joy is a profound apologetic. I once heard a missionary report on his work among a small people group in Africa. Those among the group who converted and are Christians are known as "the people who sing." When someone in their group wants to express their confession of Christ, they don't say, "I want to become a Christian." They say, "I want to sing." Among a people who have suffered terrible atrocities, decades-long strife, and conditions of rank poverty, the Christians sing because of their joy in Christ. Those Christians stand out, and the people around them ask for a reason for the hope that is in them (1 Peter 3:15).

What if we were a people of purity? And what if our purity caused people to ask us for a reason for the hope that is within us? John knew exactly what he was trying to tell us when he said if we have this hope, we purify ourselves. This idea of living as a people of purity in this moment is a very powerful apologetic.

We are living in hope and in purity, not in a vacuum and not in an hermetically sealed environment. We live in this world.

While he was in a six-by-nine-foot prison cell in Nazi Germany, Dietrich Bonhoeffer said, "The difference between the Christian hope of resurrection and the mythological hope is that the former sends a man back to his life on earth in a wholly new way."[4] The hope that derived from mythology was not hope; it was escapism. It was about getting out. The Christian hope, on the other hand, sends us right back in. But we are sent back into the world in a wholly new way and commissioned to live in a wholly new way. We are sent into the world to live holy and pure lives.

We don't get to choose the world in which we live. We don't get to choose the times in which we live. But in the place and time where we live, we are called to be faithful disciples.

Our time is a time when the ground beneath our feet is shifting. That does not give us a pass on engaging the world. Our time may very soon be a time of hostility. That does not give us a pass, either. We could even simply complain of how difficult it is to live according to a Christian ethic in the twenty-first century. That complaint does not give us a pass to get out from under our obligation. We can go right back to the recurring themes of the New Testament Epistles, especially the later ones. Christ endured. Look to Christ. You can endure.

At one point while he was in that Nazi prison cell, Bonhoeffer said, "This world must not be prematurely written off." If our confidence is in hope, it's not escapism. It's not disillusionment. It's also not naive.

We must live as Christians in this world and in this moment. We can't wax nostalgic for a bygone era that we wish was still present. We live in the moment in which God has placed us.

The early centuries of the church saw both sides of the cultural context. The early church before Constantine existed during a time of hostility and persecution. After Constantine, the early church enjoyed a time of privilege. Each period had its unique challenges and opportunities for Christians who sought to live as faithful disciples. Paul knew contentment both in times of want and need and in times of plenty (Phil. 4:10–13).

The same is true for situations in which we find ourselves. Whether in a hostile environment or whether in a privileged and friendly environment, we still have the challenge to be a faithful disciple. We may very well be leaving the familiar, navigable waters of a friendly environment, and we may very well be on the cusp of entering hostile territory. Will we engage the world as faithful disciples, or will we write the world off? Or, worse yet, will we cower and cave? There is the danger that the salt loses its saltiness and the danger that the lamp gets hidden under the basket.

Creatively Maladjusted

In the end of a sermon on Romans 12:1–2, Martin Luther King Jr. used the expression "creatively maladjusted." He turned to examples from Scripture to explain what he meant by this phrase. Shadrach, Meshach, and Abednego were creatively maladjusted people. Daniel was a creatively maladjusted person. Paul was a creatively maladjusted person. King informs us that maladjusted people suffer. They are marginalized and persecuted. Since the creatively maladjusted are outside the mainstream and since they challenge the status quo, the mainstream and the status quo return the favor by persecuting and oppressing the maladjusted. King tells us, "Christianity has always insisted that the cross we bear precedes the crown we wear. To be a Christian, one must take up his cross, with all of its difficulties and tragedy-packed content and carry it until that very cross leaves its marks upon us."[5]

There is one phrase in 1 John 1:1–3 that I left out back in our discussion. In 3:1b, John writes, "The reason why the world does not know us is that it did not know him." Christ came into this world and this world rejected Him. Bonhoeffer comments that the world pushed Christ all the way out and onto the cross. John is giving us something extremely helpful for our moment. Of course, the world at the time of Christ knew Him and the world since knows Him. What John means when he says they did not know Him is that the world did not know Him as Christ the Lord; they did not have a relationship with Him. The world did not accept Him. They considered Him an outcast.

So also, the world does not know Christians. The world does not accept Christians but rejects us and considers us outcasts. Now we know why John holds out hope to encourage us. Now we know why John exhorts us to be pure. Now we know why John tells us to rest in our identity as children of God. We are transformed.

Romans 12 speaks of two paths: conformity or conviction. The first appears to be the easy road, the road well traveled. The world knows those who conform. They applaud and celebrate those who conform. The other path is not so easy and, consequently, the not so well traveled. But those who take the lesser-traveled road have good company. The road of conviction can be lonely—it will get lonelier in the decades to come. There is One on that road, however, and that makes all the difference. We are Christ's disciples. We follow our Master. John was both warning us and comforting us when he said, "The reason why the world does not know us is that it did not know him."

Then King brings his sermon to a close by putting a series of crucial questions before his audience:

> Will we continue to march to the drumbeat of conformity and respectability, or will we listen to the beat of a more distant drum? Will we move to its echoing sounds? Will we march only to the music of time, or will we, risking criticism and abuse, march to the soul-saving music of eternity? More than ever before, we are today challenged by the words of yesterday, "Be not conformed to this world, but be transformed by the renewing of your mind."[6]

The pressures will be there to conform to culture. Will we be creatively maladjusted and, through the renewing of our mind, live a transformed life? A transformed life stands for purity in a world of cultural decadence. A transformed life knows joy during trying times. A transformed life has hope, even in the face of cynicism. A transformed life takes the Bible seriously, even radically, in a world that tunes out and rejects an ancient voice.

King is quite helpful here in calling us to be creatively maladjusted and not merely maladjusted. In his book *The Conviction to Lead*, Al Mohler declares, "To lead with conviction is to seize the role of the teacher with energy, determination, and even excitement. What could be better than seeing people learn to receive and embrace the right beliefs, seeing those beliefs and truths take hold, and then watching the organization move into action on the basis of those beliefs?" He then speaks of the urgent need for leaders, leaders who "are not satisfied until every individual understands the mission, embraces it, and brings others into it."[7] That will require some creativity on our part.

This is not retreat. This is not cynicism. This is not escapism. This is a recognition of the terrain, alongside a deeply felt and profoundly urgent call to proclaim the gospel. This is a call to be a people of confidence and to be a people of conviction—before and in the world.

A Time for Conviction

Someday, we will be like Him. That's our hope. But it's not a hope that we put on the shelf, and it's not a hope that sends us into a cave. It's a hope that sends us into the world with confidence. We can be confident in God, confident in His Word, confident in Christ, confident in the gospel, and confident in hope.

In the AD 90s, Diocletian ruled as emperor over Rome. His cruelty rivaled that of Nero. He insisted that he be worshiped as a god. Christians, of course, could not participate in the rituals of this emperor cult. That left them vulnerable, and that vulnerability led to persecution. It is likely that John's exile to the island of Patmos directly resulted from Diocletian's edicts. John refused to bow.

John wrote Revelation during this time, many scholars believe. Also around this time, an early church figure named Clement, serving as bishop at Rome, sent a letter to the church at Corinth. Clement opens his letter by referring to "the sudden and successive calamitous events." Persecution rolled over the church like wave after relentless wave. Clement wrote to comfort them and to exhort them to stand firm. Near the middle of his letter, he simply reminds the believers at Corinth that Christ is our leader and we are His soldiers.

Diocletian's edict and the persecution that followed served to press an urgent question to the church. This question was there at the very beginning. It was there at the events surrounding the incarnation when Herod ruled. It was there when the soldier drew his sword in the garden of Gethsemane, and it was there all along the excruciating and agonizing road to the cross. The question never left the early decades of the church or even the early centuries of the church. The question was this: Caesar or Christ?

Diocletian's edict made that question palpable, even visceral. Statues of him were sent all over the empire. On appointed days, feasts were held, and all of the populace had to pass before the cast image of Diocletian and bow before him as god. It was very clear: Caesar or Christ?

The truth is that question is always there. It is always before us, before the church in every age of the past. The question is before us in our time today, and it will be in front of the church in the ages to come. Who is Lord? When the Apostles and the believers in the pages of the New Testament answered that Christ is Lord and Caesar is not, ramifications followed. That decision had consequences. They did not let the temporal consequences overshadow the eternal ones. The author of Hebrews reminds the believers that they had "endured a hard struggle with sufferings, sometimes being publicly exposed to reproach and affliction, and sometimes being partners with those so treated" (Heb. 10:32–33).

Then he declares in 10:35: "Do not throw away your confidence, which has a great reward."

When the question is put to us, Caesar or Christ, may we be among those who don't shrink back. May we take our stand alongside the first-century church and the church through the centuries. May we not throw away our confidence.

From this singular point of the lordship of Christ came the church's confidence. And also from this point came the church's convictions. Chris Larson, my colleague at Ligonier Ministries, recently made the statement, "The future belongs to Christians of conviction."

This is a time for conviction. This is a time for confidence.

NOTES

Chapter One

1 Michelle Hamilton, "The Visionary: Henry Wanyoike," *Runner's World*, January/February 2015, 78–79.

2 Rob Bell, Super Soul Sunday, OWN, February 15, 2015.

3 Antonin Scalia, Dissenting Opinion, *Obergefell v. Hodges*, June 26, 2015. The full quote is: "The Supreme Court of the United States has descended from the disciplined legal reasoning of John Marshall and Joseph Story to the mystical aphorisms of the fortune cookie."

4 Jerome, Letter 127, "To Principia," (412) *The Fathers of the Church.*

5 Augustine, *The City of God*, trans. Marcus Dods (New York: The Modern Library, 1993), 3.

6 Ibid., 864.

Chapter Two

1 On Martin Luther's "A Mighty Fortress Is Our God," see Stephen J. Nichols, *Martin Luther: A Guided Tour of His Life and Thought*, revised and expanded edition (Philipsburg, N.J.: P&R, 2017) 179–94.

2 On Eric Liddell, see Duncan Hamilton, *For the Glory: Eric Liddell's Journey from Olympic Champion to Modern Martyr* (New York: Penguin, 2016).

3 For commentaries on Isaiah, see Alec Motyer, *The Prophecy of Isaiah: An Introduction & Commentary* (Downers Grove, Ill.: InterVarsity Press, 1993) and Derek W.H. Thomas, *God Delivers: Isaiah Simply Explained* (Welwyn: Evangelical Press, 1993).

4 Matthew Henry Bible Commentary, Isaiah 40:27.

5 "The Martyrdom of Polycarp," *The Fathers of the Church.*

6 John Calvin, *Commentaries, Volume 15, Isaiah, Part III.*

Chapter Three

1 For a current defense of the authority of Scripture, see John MacArthur, ed., *The Inerrant Word: Biblical, Historical, Theological, and Pastoral Perspectives* (Wheaton, Ill.: Crossway, 2016).

2 Some of the material in this section and the next previously appeared in Stephen J. Nichols, "The Bible Really Is God's Word," Bible Gateway Blog, April 9, 2015, www.biblegateway.com/blog/2015/04/the-bible-really-is-gods-word.

3 Peter Martyr Vermigli in Richard Muller, ed., *Post Reformation Reformed Dogmatics, Volume 2* (Grand Rapids, Mich.: Baker, 2003), 323.

4 Jonathan Edwards, Sermon on 1 Corinthians 2:11–13, "Ministers Not to Preach Their Own Wisdom, but the Wisdom of God," May 7, 1740, in Richard A. Bailey and Gregory A. Wills, *The Salvation of Souls* (Wheaton, Ill.: Crossway, 2002), 121.

5 Jonathan Edwards, Sermon on Micah 2:11, "The Kind of Preaching People Want," November 1733, in *The Salvation of Souls*, 60–62.

6 Jeremiah Burroughs, *The Rare Jewel of Christian Contentment* (Edinburgh, Scotland: Banner of Truth, 1964, repr.).

Chapter Four

1 See Stephen J. Nichols, *Martin Luther's 95 Theses* (Philipsburg, N.J.: P&R, 2017).

2 *Luther's Works*: Volume 32, 112–13.

3 Dietrich Bonhoeffer, "Jesus Christ and the Essence of Christianity," December 11, 1928, in *Dietrich Bonhoeffer Works, Volume 10* (Minneapolis: Fortress, 2008), 357.

4 John Calvin, *Institutes of the Christian Religion*, ed. John T. McNeill, trans. Ford Lewis Battles, Vol. 2 (Philadelphia: Westminster, 1960), 1485.

5 Ibid., 1508.

6 Ibid., 1521.

7 Ibid., 1521.

8 To Jacob Probst, January 17, 1546, in *The Letters of Martin Luther*, ed. and trans. Margaret A. Currie (London: Macmillan, 1908), 468.

Chapter Five

1 George Yancey and David A. Williamson, *So Many Christians, So Few Lions: Is There Christianophobia in the United Sates?* (Lanham, Md.: Rowman & Littlefield, 2015) 63, 64, 70, 72.

2 Francis Turretin, *Institutes of Elenctic Theology, Three Volumes*, ed. James T. Dennison Jr., trans. George Musgrave Giger (Philipsburg, N.J.: P&R, 1994), Vol. 2: 724.

3 Johnny Cash, *The Man in White: A Novel about the Apostle Paul* (Nashville, Tenn.: WestBow, 1986).

4 Jonathan Edwards, *The Works of Jonathan Edwards, Volume 9: The History of the Work of Redemption,* ed. John F. Wilson (New Haven, Conn.: Yale University Press, 1989), 113.

5 Ibid., 524.

6 Ibid., 526.

Chapter Six

1 "Heaven Is a World of Love," in *The Works of Jonathan Edwards, Volume 8: Ethical Writings*, ed. Paul Ramsey (New Haven, Conn.: Yale University Press, 1989) 366–97.

2 R.C. Sproul, *The Holiness of God*, 25th Anniversary Edition (Orlando, Fla.: Ligonier Ministries, 2010), 35.

3 Martin Luther "Theses for the Heidelberg Disputation, 1518" in *Martin Luther's Basic Theological Writings*, ed. Timothy F. Lull (Minneapolis: Fortress Press, 1989), 32.

4 Dietrich Bonhoeffer to Eberhard Bethge, June 27, 1944, in *Letters and Papers from Prison*, ed. Eberhard Bethge (New York: Touchstone, 1997), 366–67.

5 Martin Luther King Jr., "Transformed Nonconformist," in *American Sermons: The Pilgrims to Martin Luther King, Jr.* (New York: The Library of America, 1999), 848.

6 Ibid., 848.

7 R. Albert Mohler Jr., *The Conviction to Lead: 25 Principles for Leadership that Matters* (Minneapolis: Bethany House, 2012), 73.

INDEX

ABOUT THE AUTHOR

Dr. Stephen J. Nichols is president of Reformation Bible College in Sanford, Fla., and chief academic officer and a teaching fellow for Ligonier Ministries. He earned his PhD from Westminster Theological Seminary and earned master's degrees from West Chester University in Pennsylvania and Westminster Theological Seminary.

Dr. Nichols is a prolific writer who has written, contributed to, or edited more than twenty books on church history, biblical doctrine, and practical theology. Among his books are *For Us and for Our Salvation, Jesus Made in America, Martin Luther: A Guided Tour of His Life and Thought, Heaven on Earth: Capturing Jonathan Edwards's Vision of Living in Between, The Reformation,* and *Peace.* He is also the coeditor for the Theologians on the Christian Life series from Crossway, and he hosts the podcast *5 Minutes in Church History.*

Dr. Nichols and his wife, Heidi, have three children. They live in Sanford.